Court Scenes

Priscilla Coleman
and Paul Cheston

Court Scenes

The court art of Priscilla Coleman
with commentary by Paul Cheston

Wildy Simmonds & Hill Publishing
London

Images © 2010 Priscilla Coleman
Text © 2010 Paul Cheston

Court Scenes

First published in 2010 by
Wildy, Simmonds & Hill Publishing Ltd
58 Carey Street, London WC2A 2JB, UK

Designed and set by Oblong Creative Ltd, Wetherby
Printed and bound by Green Light Print Solutions Ltd

British Library Cataloguing-in-Publication Data:
A catalogue record for this book is available from The British
Library

ISBN 9780854900398

Contents

Preface

I first met Priscilla when she was thrown fully clothed into a swimming pool by ITN veteran Colin Baker. Coolly she climbed out of the pool and stripped off to reveal she had had the foresight to wear a swimming costume underneath. A formidable woman, I thought, and ever since that poolside party – at the Rock Hotel, Gibraltar in September 1988 during a break in the inquest into the SAS shootings – nothing has altered my initial impression.

For the next 20 years we shared pressbox seats at the Old Bailey and the High Court, and in courts from Cardiff to Ipswich and Preston to Winchester as well as inquests, courts martials and trials overseas.

Whenever I've rushed from court to file for early edition deadlines, I've found Priscilla with her box of crayons pouring over her canvas laid out on a pressroom table, if she's lucky, or, in the last resort, on her hands and knees scrambling on the floor. Yet while I'm yelling down the phone to a copytaker or hammering the keys of a laptop, Priscilla maintains an enviable serenity and sang-froid, not to mention her usual charm and courtesy so traditional to the native of the Lone Star state. Inexperienced TV producers, over-officious court clerks and distracted reporters jogging her drawing arm are all treated to her warmest, most patient smile. Whatever the pressure, whatever the rush, Priscilla will have her pictures ready for the next ITN bulletin. How does she do that?

There is a widespread misunderstanding among those who see Priscilla's pictures on TV or in the newspapers that artists can sketch as much as they like in court. As lawyers know, far from taking a palette and easel into the public gallery, any attempt at photography, drawings or visual representations is strictly *verboten*.

Artists have to memorise in court the colours, shades, clothing, facial mannerisms and physical idiosyncrasies then go out and draw a likeness from memory ... against the clock.

How beetled was the defendant's brow? How much grey hair was sticking out from beneath the judge's wig? Were prosecution counsel's eyebrows really so bushy?

It's a tough job, particularly when you add in the backdrop, the banks of bewigged barristers and important faces in the public gallery.

Tough jobs need generous and hard-working colleagues for support.

In producing this book nothing could have been achieved without the patience of Brian Hill of Wildy Simmonds and Hill Publishing and the hours of work by Steve Maisey the number one freelance photographer at the Old Bailey.

Many ITN reporters and producers have been a beacon of support, but particularly Colin Baker, the late Terry Lloyd, Harry Smith, Libby Wiener, Shulie Ghosh, Anne Lingley, Nigel Hancock, David Mannion, David Stanley and so many cameramen and women.

David St George kindly showed Priscilla round the Old Bailey on her first day.

Thanks also to Jackie Henderson of the Art Library, who deals with Priscilla's paintings in New Zealand.

Peter Worley and his staff at the Newgate gallery of 66 Clerkenwell Road, deserve great thanks for framing and promoting so many sketches. Thanks also to Kevin Fisher at the Newgate Gallery. Priscilla's work is available through Getty Images.

Equally, when memories have threatened to dim, the support of Adrian Shaw of the *Daily Mirror*, Pat Clarke and Shenai Raif of the Press Association, and Sue Clough of the *Daily Telegraph*, have been invaluable.

Paul Cheston
Priscilla Coleman
24 September 2009

R. *v* Damien Hanson, Elliot White

One of the most harrowing Old Bailey scenes of 2005 was the sight of attempted murder victim Homeyra Monckton hobbling into the witness box on a stick.

She had been stabbed twice in the back and left for dead alongside her husband John dying in the hallway of their Chelsea home.

Robbers Damien Hanson and Elliot White had burst into the house disguised as postmen delivering a parcel.

Mrs Monckton, 46, would have died too but for her nine-year-old daughter Isobel who dialled 999.

Pale-faced and dressed in black she entered court from the judge's entrance to avoid the awkward steps to the witness box.

Questioned by Richard Horwell for the Crown, she was unable to prevent tears running down her cheeks as she relived her personal pain and the sight of her City banker husband fighting for his life.

She told how she was stabbed trying to reach the panic alarm and lay bleeding copiously as the balaclava'd raiders demanded her jewellery.

"I took off my rings and earrings and watch but I don't remember handing them to him because I was bleeding a lot," she told the jury in a frail voice.

"He asked me for money and I pointed out to him where my handbag was.

"They were evil, they destroyed our lives, I just felt sheer panic – panic and fear."

Mrs Monckton was barely conscious when paramedics arrived and was to lose seven pints of blood.

Mr Justice Calvert-Smith handed down life sentences for Hanson, who had been on an early release scheme from a 12-year sentence, for murder, attempted murder and robbery.

He said Hanson, known as "Devil child" had only narrowly averted a "life means life" tariff and imposed a 36-year minimum.

White, a cocaine and heroin addict who was convicted of manslaughter and wounding with intent, was also jailed for life with an 18-year minimum.

R. *v* Roy Whiting

Dirty, scruffy van driver Roy Whiting had snatched a young girl for his sexual pleasure before but having released her he was caught and jailed.

In prison he vowed that next time the little girl he targetted would not be so lucky. That happy little innocent target turned out to be Sarah Payne.

The jury at Lewes Crown Court in 2001 heard her brother Lee say he had been playing with his eight year-old sister in a corn field near Littlehampton on the Sussex coast when she popped through a gap in the hedge.

When Lee, 13, arrived he saw a van driver with yellowish teeth grinning and waving at him as he roared off with, unknown to the boy, Sarah hidden in the back.

Her body was found two weeks later 12 miles away in a field near Pulborough.

Knowing Whiting's record – he had abducted a nine-year-old girl in Crawley six years earlier – police was on his doorstep within 24 hours and arrested him in the van which contained critical forensic evidence.

Whiting pleaded not guilty, denied everything and even told the jury: "I have nothing to hide and I'm telling the truth."

His every step and gesture in court was followed by Sarah's parents Michael and Sara, leader of the Sarah's Law campaign to give local residents the right to know when a paedophile released from prison settles in their neighbourhood.

On the guilty verdict Mr Justice Curtis told Whiting he would never be released from his life sentence.

"You are indeed an evil man," the judge told him, "You turned your van into a moving prison for Sarah."

R. *v* Charles Ingram, Diana Ingram, Tecwen Whittock

Since March 2003 Major Charles Ingram has been dogged in the streets wherever he goes by the sound of strangers coughing and jeering.

It is the price of the fame he never sought, the notoriety of being caught trying to cheat in front of a TV audience of millions, rather than the fame he wanted as the country's first ever £1 million quiz show winner.

The *Who Wants To Be A Millionaire* trial was a ratings winner from the first episode and kept newspaper readers and TV bulletin viewers amused no end.

As Nicholas Hilliard told the jury at Southwark Crown Court in his opening speech, Ingram, his wife Diana and Tecwen Whittock tried to win the bumper prize by developing a system of coughing from the audience to indicate the right answer.

Ingram first had to win his place in the hot seat opposite quizmaster Chris Tarrant and then fit the coughing to the multiple answer questions to hit the jackpot.

Which he duly did until programme makers checked the video tape of the show, rumbled what had been going on, cancelled the cheque and called in the police.

The strength of the plan was its audacity, the drawback was that, with hindsight, it was hilariously obvious what was going on.

When the tape, which at that time had never been broadcast, was played in court, Judge Geoffrey Rivlin stopped proceedings, sent out the jury and warned that if the laughter from the public gallery and press box did not stop he would clear the court.

Giving evidence Tarrant (pictured) said he was too pre-occupied in running the show to notice the coughing in the studio.

Other witness said the Ingrams had a terrible row in the dressing room after the show when a normal winning couple would have been drinking champagne with unbridled joy.

Apparently Mrs Ingram was pointing out to her husband in her blunt fashion that the original plan had been only to win a more modest, albeit substantial, prize to avoid the inevitable scrutiny of landing the biggest payout in TV quiz show history.

Unfortunately once the bait was dangled the major could not resist pressing on to the end.

The judge took a merciful view imposing suspended sentences for procuring the execution of a valuable security by deception.

The Ingrams fought on and succeeded in getting their fines and the order to contribute to prosecution costs reduced on appeal. But their convictions remained and their fate – like the Hamiltons – is to be famous for being greedy and courtroom losers.

R. *v* Matthew Simmons

The flying kung-fu kick by Manchester United football star Eric Cantona on a spectator was a shocking TV image but his victim that day was to later launch his own violent attack in court.

Cantona was charged with assault but double-glazing fitter Matthew Simmons also faced the court for threatening behaviour in sparking the incident during United's match with Crystal Palace at Selhurst Park.

When Croydon magistrate Mary Parkinson found him guilty, Simmons threw himself across desks in the well of the court and grabbed the throat of prosecutor Jeffrey McCann.

It was such a sudden flash of violence, not just unexpected but unprecedented in the normally sleepy court, that press and policemen were momentarily frozen.

Eventually six officers pulled Simmons off and dragged him to the cells, the demented football fan still screaming "I'm innocent."

Poor Mr McCann, 56, had his collar and tie scragged but was otherwise unhurt. The Simmons case was his last, and unexpectedly memorable, prosecution before retirement.

Sportingly he accepted Simmons' subsequent apology and declined to press charges but the magistrates jailed the 21-year-old thug for contempt of court on top of £700 in fines and costs on the threatening behaviour charge and banned him from every football ground in the country.

A few months after the Palace match in 1995, Cantona pleaded guilty to common assault on Simmons and was sentenced to two weeks' imprisonment cut on appeal to 120 hours commmunity service. He was later suspended from football by the FA for nine months.

In the Premiership game Cantona had been sent off and was walking back to the changing rooms when Simmons ran to the front of the terraces and, according to witnesses, provoked the Frenchman with a stream of racist and obscene abuse.

In court Simmons tried to claim he was only "teasing" Cantona saying: "Off you go Cantona, it's an early bath for you."

His later outburst against Mr McCann showed just how laughably unlikely that explanation was.

R. *v* Peter Bryan

In a grubby bedsit in Walthamstow a convicted killer and cannibal sautées the brains of a victim in a frying pan with a little butter.

This is not some cheap Hannibal Lecter-style film script but evidence at the Old Bailey.

Hours before hacking his friend Brian Cherry to death, Peter Bryan had attended an East London mental hospital and was allowed to go home.

Even after his arrest he continued his spree killing a fellow inmate at Broadmoor.

Later when being examined by a psychiatrist, he told the doctor: "Mmm, you seem a brainy chap, and quite slim, I think I could take you."

Bryan had killed first in 1994 and was sent to Rampton maximum security hospital. He passed through the system each time moving to a lower security level until, in 2004, he was in an open ward as an "informal patient."

He started killing again and admitted he wanted eight victims to qualify as a serial killer and enjoyed the buzz of sexual excitement from these violent deaths and voodoo rituals.

A cannibal has rarely sat in the dock at the Bailey and Bryan, 36, was calm and uncomplaining although clearly heavily sedated and flanked by five hefty male nurses.

He admitted two counts of manslaughter on the grounds of diminished responsiblity and was sentenced to life imprisonment by Judge Giles Forrester.

"You killed because it gave you a thrill and a feeling of power when you ate flesh. Life imprisonment should mean the rest of your natural life," said the judge.

Abu Hamza
Belmarsh
magistrates Ct.

R. *v* Abu Hamza

Abu Hamza's one-eyed scowl was the face of militant Islam for the tabloid press which dubbed him the "hook-handed cleric of hate".

The fact he lived off benefits and delivered his ranting speeches in the street after his powerbase, the Finsbury Park mosque, was closed to him, added to the red top message that he should be denounced for what he looked like and not what he was trying to do.

In fact Hamza was far more than this press-painted pantomime figure. He was and remains a very dangeorus man.

In January 2006 he finally went on trial at the Old Bailey for soliciting the murder of Jews and non-believers, inciting racial hatred and possessing a terrorist manual.

David Perry QC was given the difficult task of separating the specific crimes, mostly on taped sermons to his followers, from any suggestion that Islam itself was on trial.

Hamza, 47 sat in the dock in tunic and trousers but without his hook, no doubt for security reasons.

Outwardly he cut a disinterested figure acknowledging his various names, he had several aliases, with a dismissive gesture.

When he came to give evidence he answered Edward Fitzgerald QC's questions with a modest voice brimming with reasonableness which was far from the strident, aggressive and dogmatic tones of the video tapes.

He was jailed for seven years. Later police released photos of the vast arsenal of weaponry seized in a raid on the mosque when under Hamza's iron grip, which many of Europe's most fanatical terrorists had used as a base.

After the conviction Hamza prepared for another long legal battle, this time against extradition to the United States where he faced far more serious charges including helping to plot a 1998 terrorist attack in Yemen which had left three Britons dead.

R. *v* John Terry, Jodie Morris, Desmond Byrne

By August 2002 the public had become heartily tired of stories of over-paid Premiership footballers, swathed in jewellry drinking and brawling in the streets.

There had been a number of high profile trials and public pressure was mounting for convictions.

One of the most serious cases involved John Terry, then a young Chelsea player, who was accused of using a bottle with intent to inflict grievous bodily harm.

Now Terry is England captain and a role model but at that trial in Middlesex Guildhall Crown Court he faced the threat of up to eight years in prison.

Terry had become involved in a fracas with Jodie Morris, then also a young Chelsea player, and Des Byrne, of Wimbledon, at the Wellington Club in Knightsbridge.

They were drinking B-52s, a potent mix of Kahlua, Baileys and Cointreau, a fight broke out and the police were called. Terry said he had acted only in self defence.

Terry was represented by Desmond de Silva QC, who established in cross examining the doorman and alleged victim Trevor Thirlwell that the club had been operating outside its licence.

Thirlwell admitted that he was not licensed as a club bouncer by the local council and that he had lied to the police.

De Silva pointed out that if the footballers had not started the trouble and had indeed acted only in self-defence the club's licence would have been in serious jeopardy.

Terry gave evidence, often breaking into tears under the pressure of knowing his career was on the line.

When the jury retired he bought a packed bag in case he ended the day in prison.

Terry and Morris were cleared of all charges and Byrne found guilty only of a lesser charge.

The threat of prison transformed Terry's life on and off the pitch. He is now one of England's best and highest paid footballers.

Court 35 High Court of Justice
Chancery Division

James Price QC questions Catherine Zeta Jones
for Hello magazine Michael Douglas in foreground
Before Mr. Justice Lindsay
Monday Feb. 10th 2003
Douglas & anr v Hello ors Ltd.

for ITN

OK! v Hello and others

Hollywood glamour is a rare visitor to the High Court and the arrival of Catherine Zeta-Jones and her husband Michael Douglas did not disappoint.

They were driven straight into the judges' car park in the back of a black Mercedes with blacked-out windows.

The seven-month pregnant actress was dressed all in black and radiated maternal charm and not a little *grandeur*.

In a peculiar accent mixing California and the Gower peninsula she told how she felt "violated, distressed and angry to this day" that the first photographs of her wedding had appeared in the wrong celebrity magazine.

The Oscar-winning stars had married in New York in November 2000 amid security which would have done credit to a Cold War summit.

They sold the rights to exclusive pictures to *OK!* for £1 million but before it could publish *Hello* ran some snatched shots taken by English paparazzo Rupert Thorpe who had infiltrated the reception.

As a result *OK!* sued *Hello* for breach of confidentiality and contract and the Douglases lent their support and claimed their privacy had been invaded.

In court both stars stressed the importance of privacy above money, after all, said Zeta-Jones, they didn't consider "£1 million to be a lot of money."

Mr Justice Lindsay found, on most matters, in favour of *OK!* but this was far from the end of the matter.

The Appeal Court overturned the decision and found in favour of *Hello* but this too was finally reversed by the Law Lords.

R. *v* Muktar Said Ibrahim and others

Muktar Said Ibrahim was the leader of an al-Qaeda cell of would-be suicide bombers and knew how to keep a cool head.

In days of evidence from the witness box he rarely appeared ruffled, even when faced with the overwhelming evidence against him and his fellow terrorists, and calmly batted back the most awkward of questions.

Known as "the emir", his serenity came from the strength of his power base among like-minded people and his conviction of righteousness in line with his view of his faith.

He seemed wholly unpreturbed that his great scheme to achieve martyrdom by blowing up London's tube trains and a bus has failed dismally.

Exactly two weeks after the devastation in London on 7 July 2005 Ibrahim, an Ethiopian who had been in Britain 15 years, led his troops onto the tube network all armed with potentially deadly homemade explosives.

He himself headed from Stockwell on the Northern Line to Bank then caught a no 26 bus where he tried to detonate his bomb between Shoreditch High Street and Hackney Road.

Like all the devices they mercifully failed to detonate and Ibrahim was arrested a few days later, somewhat embarrassingly stripped to the waist with his arms flung high on the walkway of flats in West London.

At Woolwich Crown Court the gang's defence was that they knew the bombs would not go off and they were only trying to raise awareness of the plight of Muslims worldwide.

Ibrahim, Ramzi Mohammed, Yassin Omar – who had fled to Birmingham in a burkha after his abortive operation – and Hussein Osman were all convicted of conspiracy to murder and were jailed for life.

Mr Justice Fulford imposed minimum terms of 40 years.

The jury was unable to agree verdicts on two other defendants, who later pleaded guilty to lesser charges.

Tom Cruise *v* Express Newspapers

Tom Cruise was Hollywood's biggest star and in 1998 he and his wife Nicole Kidman topped the celebrity couple A list.

When the *Express on Sunday* magazine published lies about his marriage and his faith he was going to have his day in court – even if it was to last just a few minutes.

Far from the cinematic he-man, the star of *Top Gun* and *Mission Impossible* cut a slim and diminutive figure with a pony tail when he slipped into court 13 at the High Court with his counsel and American lawyers.

He cheerfully signed a host of autographs for court staff – the ushers' grapevine had been red hot and a queue quickly built up.

When Mr Justice Eady entered, Cruise's QC George Carman read out a short agreed statement which Patrick Moloney QC for the Express group confirmed. The false allegations were formally withdrawn and apologies tendered.

And that was that. Cruise and Miss Kidman were £100,000 richer from the libel damages, which they donated to charity, and the Express was also ordered to pay estimated costs of £150,000.

The stars had sued for libel over allegations that their then seven-year marriage was a "mere business arrangement or under the orders of the Church of Scientology or as a cover-up for the homosexuality of one or both of them."

The magazine went on to accuse Cruise of being sterile and impotent and telling lies whenever he denied the allegations.

The couple's two adopted children, Isabella then aged five, and Connor, three, were said to have been rescued from poor conditions only "following some dictate of fashion in uptown Los Angeles."

Outside court, surrounded by photographers, Cruise spoke of "the vicious lies" which had caused him and his family so much distress and how he had gone to court reluctantly to protect his children.

Miss Kidman was not present. At the time she was appearing in *The Blue Room* in the West End which was famously described by a critic – in a phrase since much repeated – as "pure theatrical viagra."

R. *v* Joyti de Laurey and others

"She had the chance to live the life of a millionaire and snapped it up, and who wouldn't?" asked Jeremy Dein QC, defending the wonderfully flamboyant but ultimately crooked personal secretary Joyti de Laurey.

The joy of the de Laurey trial was the way it placed everyone of us in the interesting position of asking ourselves: "Well what would I have done?"

De Laurey, 35, worked for senior bankers at Goldman Sachs and was undoubtedly good at her job.

She became indispensable to American husband and wife Ron Beller and Jennifer Moses and then to even wealthier Edward Scott Mead.

The problem was she quickly realised they were so rich they actually didn't know how much money they had.

So when she started raking off bits here and there they didn't initially notice. But, inevitably, it got out of hand and she was eventually rumbled having stolen £4.3 million which she spent, naturally enough, on luxury cars, a string of properties, expensive holidays and Cartier diamonds.

De Laurey ended up in the dock at Southwark Crown Court in 2004 charged with 20 counts of deception.

Alongside her was her then husband Anthony – who arrived at court every day bizzarely dressed in a hat, scarf, overcoat, dark glasses and sporting a full beard – and her mother Dr Devi Schahhou who were both accused of assisting her in spending and laundering the proceeds of crime.

If the jury did ask themselves the question of what they would have done in her place, they put it all aside to find her guilty and she was sentenced to seven years. Her husband and mother were also found guilty.

While still in prison her story was dramatised on television and her part played by the rather more glamorous Meera Syal.

Ironically on her release on parole in 2007, de Laurey was reported to have moved into a two-bedroom flat in Cheam, Surrey she had bought at the height of her illegal spending spree. Goldman Sachs had not attempted to claim it back.

R. *v* Ken Dodd

It is difficult to imagine now, but in June 1989 one of Britain's best-loved comedians seriously feared he was going to jail.

Ken Dodd faced seven charges of cheating the Inland Revenue over 14 years and four further counts of false accounting between 1982 and 1988.

Just two years earlier Lester Piggott, the nation's most famous jockey often referred to as the housewives' favourite, was sent down after pleading guilty to similar charges.

Dodd did not hide his fears but his trial at Liverpool Crown Court turned into a triumph which made him even more popular and reinvigorated his career.

Ironically if his counsel George Carman QC had his way there would have been no trial. He applied for the case to be stayed on the grounds of Dodd's potentially fatal heart condition.

The comedian, who gave his age as 61 but looked 81, appeared in court on the first day with deadened eyes, sickly pallour and heavily furrowed brow.

But Mr Justice Waterhouse refused the application when fresh medical tests found Dodd fit to stand trial.

The next day as Brian Leveson QC opened the Crown's case, Dodd was transformed his eyes now bright and his face, if not characteristically full of mischief, at least alert.

Leveson, who looked like an accountant with his short, serious and bespectacled appearance, told the jury Dodd had acrued around £500,000 in off shore bank accounts which he failed to declare to the taxman and kept £336,000 hidden in shoeboxes under a bed and in cupboards at various properties he owned around Liverpool.

He accused the comedian of lying to the Inland Revenue inspectors and committing "a tax fraud … on a grand scale."

But Carman, aided by a now vibrant veteran comic playing in front of a home audience, painted a different picture. Dodd spent just £470 a year on clothes and only £26 a week on food. He had genuinely, if erroneously, believed all his off-shore savings were tax free.

Examination in chief turned into a master class in taking a client sympathetically through his evidence, and winning the confidence of a jury which regularly hooted with laughter.

Successfully Carman showed how Dodd was guilty of nothing more than being distrustful and naive with banks and accountants. "I don't have to be dishonest, I'm a successful entertainer," insisted the defendant.

Then, when under pressure in cross exdamination, he pleaded with the jury: "I am an honest man, I realised I had made a mistake. I have done nothing dishonest, mistaken maybe, but I'm not dishonest."

Remarkably, in the presence of a great comedian on rare form, the one line for which the trial is best remembered came from Carman himself.

Referring to the Crown's decision not to call Reg Hunter, who had been Dodd's accountant for 10 years, but had a criminal conviction for false accounting and was the man the defence blamed for leaving the comedian's records in such a mess, Carman told the jury: "Comedians are not chartered accountants, but sometimes chartered accountants are comedians."

Dodd was acquitted on all charges and Carman's reputation was enhanced to an even higher level. It was to be his last great criminal trial before he found further fame in the field of libel.

Coroner's inquest into the deaths of Mairead Farrell, Sean Savage and Daniel McCann

In 1987 the British Government was at war with the IRA, which was repeatedly and successfully killing soldiers and civilians in Northern Ireland, the British mainland and abroad.

An SAS squad tracked an IRA cell to southern Spain and watched as they drove onto Gibraltar and left their car in a highly sensitive area where the Royal Anglian Regiment was due to parade.

As Mairead Farrell, Sean Savage and Daniel McCann walked away the undercover soldiers – fearing the terrorists was about to detonate a bomb planted in the car – opened fire with dozens of rounds of bullets at short range in the crowded streets.

The suspects, who were on a dry run for a real bombing, turned out to be unarmed and there was no bomb in the car, although two days later a vast amount of their semtex timed to go off during the changing of the guard was found near their base over the border in Spain.

An outcry ensued and the Thatcher government was left with extremely tricky legal, diplomatic and propoganda problems at the inquest on the Rock in September the next year.

The hearing conducted by Gibraltar coroner Felix Pizzarello was held in the colony's old courthouse in swelteringly humid conditions.

John Laws QC headed the Crown's team and the wily Paddy McGrory, aided by local solicitor Chris Finch, represented the families of the dead.

MI5 officers and the soldiers involved all gave evidence from behind a screen which cordoned off the witness box in a corner of the court.

Each soldier told the jury that their principle concern as they opened fire was to save local lives, each using the phrase that the safety of the people of Gibraltar was "uppermost in my mind".

Such was the sense of secrecy and security brown wrapping paper was taped across a highly polished door behind the screen in case a witness's reflection could be seen in the public gallery.

The most controversial witness was Carmen Proetta who was looking out of her flat window and saw the shooting right beneath her.

Her account differed significantly from the soldiers' version and there were repeated attempts in the British press to rubbish her credibility, which later led to some substantial libel payouts for her.

At the end of the three week hearing the jury, deliberated long before returning verdicts of lawful killing.

However seven years later they were overturned at the European court in Strasbourg when Britain was found to have used excessive force in breach of the European Convention on Human Rights.

R. v Sion Jenkins

Three trials and two appeals over nine years and no one is any nearer proving who killed 13-year-old Billie-Jo Jenkins.

It was a horrible and savage murder, the teenager bludgeoned to death with a heavy metal tent peg on the patio of the family home in Hastings in 1997.

The man arrested was her foster father, deputy headmaster Sion Jenkins and the first day of his first trial at Lewes Crown Court opened in violence when Billie-Jo's natural father Bill managed to punch his namesake on his way into court.

East-Ender Bill, who had booked himself into a local hotel, sat in the front row of the public gallery brooding and glaring at the dock for the duration of the trial.

In the witness box Sion Jenkins said the damning microscopic specks of Billie-Jo's blood found on his clothing had come not from the attack but when he craddled her in his arms in front of his other children and an air bubble had burst through her lips.

But the powertully built teacher came over as authoritarian and dogmatic. Crucially Richard Camden Pratt QC, prosecuting, made him lose his temper. "So that's it. That's what happened when you struck Billie-Jo," he told Jenkins and the jury.

Jenkins was convicted and sentenced to life imprisonment but continued to protest his innocence.

His first appeal failed but later new evidence backed up his air-bubble defence and a second appeal succeeded.

At the retrial at the Old Bailey. Christopher Sallon QC took over the defence from Anthony Scrivenor QC and Clare Montgomery QC, and Nicholas Hilliard prosecuted in place of Camden Pratt.

For the first time Jenkins' estranged wife Lois gave evidence via a video link from her new home with their four natural children in Australasia.

She told how she had long suspected him but – unsurprisingly given it was the middle of the night Down Under – she appeared tetchy and unsympathetic.

Mrs Justice Rafferty ruled inadmissable her evidence, revealed at the appeal, that Jenkins had beaten her.

Jurors were unable to reach a verdict and at a third trial the jury was hung again leaving the Crown with no option but to call no further evidence.

Jenkins emerged from court – this time Billie-Jo's aunts managed to unload a few haymakers on him – into the arms of his new wife.

Gillian Taylforth *v* News International

Gillian Taylforth is a successful actress and a familiar face on TV. But she became a national laughing stock when she sued the *Sun* for libel.

Not only was she humiliated by defeat and left with a massive legal bill, but her name became synonymous not with acting but roadside oral sex.

More importantly it turned the tide in libel when, for the first time in the era of tabloid lies and excess, a jury backed a red-top newspaper against a celebrity.

Taylforth went to court in January 1994 over a front page story alleging she had been caught by a police officer having oral sex with partner Geoff Knights in their car.

Knights accepted a police caution but she insisted she had been merely easing his trousers during an attack of pancreatitis.

The gentlemanly and academic Michael Beloff QC was briefed to represent her in an attempt to take the high moral ground.

The *Sun*, more experienced at get-down-and-dirty libel battles, went for George Carman QC.

The case was decided by tactical errors which might have been anticipated and a ghost from her past she could never have expected.

In the witness box Taylforth's glamourous but simpering vulnerability was perfect but Knights was hopeless. A lengthy criminal record was unsavoury and his excuse for accepting a caution for something he said he had not done was unconvincing.

Then the court trooped out to the judges' car park to see the couple "prove" that oral sex in a seat belt was impossible. But they were upstaged by two young and red-faced *Sun* reporters who showed they were quite able to simulate the act even with the jury's faces pressed to the car windows.

Taylforth could still have won but for what became known as the "sausage video." Allegedly delivered anonymously to the *Sun*'s office in Wapping in mid-trial it showed a young Taylforth in girly horseplay laughing and joking about a variety of impromptu sex aids.

As a bit of fun from years ago it was harmless, but its effect on the jury was totally disastrous as it destroyed her claims to have been reduced to tears by the *Sun*'s allegations.

When the jury's verdict went against her she collapsed in court and was taken off to hospital. Drama queen or queen of drama? Defeat lent her a certain risqué reputation which does not seem to have harmed her subsequent acting career.

R. *v* Paul Gadd

Gary Glitter was charged under his real name of Paul Gadd but played remorselessly on his showbiz image.

Hoping for a "pro-celebrity" verdict from the jury he arrived at Bristol Crown Court in November 1999 in a black limo, dressed all in black as he would on stage and with a big black wig over his bald pate.

He had pleaded guilty to downloading child porn on his laptop computer which had been discovered when he had taken it for repairs at PC World.

As a result the jury, who were to decide on charges of sexually abusing a 14-young-old girl fan, knew nothing of his admitted paedophilia.

Taken through her evidence by John Royce QC, prosecuting, she told how her parents had thought him a nice pleasant man and allowed him to stay at their home. When they were out he repaid their hospitality by abusing their daughter who had hero-worshipped him.

Now 34 and a mother-of-three, she had only come forward after news of Glitter's arrest on the computer charges and, foolishly, had gone to the press first.

Trevor Burke QC, defending, took remorseless advantage of that and her understandable confusion over the passing of years and tore the poor girl's credibility to shreds.

As she left court in tears she looked over her shoulder at the dock with a beseeching glance but her former hero turned away disdainfully.

On the evidence the jury were right to clear the pop star but how did they feel when Mr Justice Butterfield ordered the second indictment to be read? Faces froze in the jury box and the public gallery where a handful of Glitter fans had been gleefully chanting "leader, leader" moments earlier.

In a stomach-turning show of self-pity and theatrical wimpering Glitter hung his head as each of the 54 charges were read out.

He was sentenced to four months and, on release, left the country in disgrace to peddle and indulge his perverted lust in a variety of far-eastern countries.

Jonathan Aitken *v The Guardian* and Granada TV

If Neil Hamilton represented the comedic venality of 1990s Tory sleeze, Jonathan Aitken's failings were far, far more serious.

Here was a senior Government minister lying to the Cabinet Secretary, Prime Minister and Parliament about accepting gifts from a foreign, if friendly, power.

But like Hamilton he brought about his own downfall, suing for libel, in his case with the preposterous bravado of taking up "the simple sword of truth."

The allegations, by the *Guardian* and ITV's *World in Action*, were that Aitken was a gun runner, pimped prostitutes for Saudi royalty and took backhanders from them. But it came down to the single issue of a night at the Ritz hotel, Paris, and who paid?

Aitken won the first round when, much to the fury of George Carman QC, the trial was heard in front of a judge sitting alone and not a jury.

In front of a benign Mr Justice Popplewell the Privy Councillor gave fluent evidence. But from the press seats, immediately opposite the witness box, there was something clearly wrong.

There was none of the smirking self confidence of Jeffrey Archer 10 years earlier, but there was a definite unease, slightly darting eyes, slightly edgy smile, the slightly quicker speech of a craven liar.

In the second week Aitken declared outside court that the following day would be "Ladies Day" when his wife Lolicia and daughter Victoria would give evidence to support his claim that Mrs Aitken had paid the Ritz bill and not the Saudi royal family.

What he didn't know was that *Guardian* reporter Owen Bowcott was digging in the cellar archives of the hotel where the Aitken *femmes* had been staying that night and it wasn't the Ritz, nor in Paris nor even France, it was in Switzerland where Victoria was attending finishing school.

Even more alarming for Aitken, British Airways staff were going through the records of flights from Heathrow to Geneva.

When the results were disclosed to the defence Aitken fled to the United States. When he failed to turn up in court Charles Gray QC asked for one day adjournment.

The next day – having announced his impending divorce from Lolicia overnight – he was again missing and Carman was able to claim another astonishing victory.

A year later Aitken stood before the Recorder of London, Michael Hyam QC, to plead guilty to perjury and attempting to pervert the course of justice. He was later jaild for 18 months.

Coroner's inquest into the deaths of Diana, Princess of Wales, and Dodi al-Fayed

For the millions who grieved around the world the death of Diana, Princess of Wales was one of the greatest tragedies of modern times.

The inquest into why and what happened in the Pont de l'Alma tunnel in Paris in August 1997 did not even start until 10 years had elapsed.

By that time the Stevens Report had concluded that the chauffeur Henri Paul was drunk and speeding at the wheel of a car he was not licensed to drive.

Mohamed Fayed, whose son Dodi also died in the car crash, remained convinced there has been an Establishment cover up of murder.

Even the preliminary hearings leading up to the full inquest provided drama, confrontation and simmering resentment across court 73 at the High Court worthy of the great controversy.

The most electric clashes were between Baroness Butler-Sloss, former head of the Family Division and first choice for the exacting task of coroner, and Michael Mansfield QC, representing Mr Fayed.

On one side a woman respected as a model judge of her time but sadly whose inquest experience was practically nil.

On the other a brilliant operator in the field whose knowledge covered a host of high profile inquests, such as the Deptford fire, the Marchioness disaster, the Stephen Lawrence murder and Stuart Lubbock's death in Michael Barrymore's swimming pool.

Their spats started over the key issue of whether a jury or the coroner alone should decide the verdict.

Lady Butler-Sloss, who had never worked before with a jury, rejected that option and Mansfield successfully overturned the decision after a judicial review.

Faced by this reverse Lady Butler-Sloss eventually stood down and was replaced by Lord Justice Scott Baker. But not before she complained to Mansfield that he was adopting a too "adversarial" approach.

The QC, furious at being lectured on the basics of one of his specialist subjects, was red faced as their argument raged for a full 40 minutes.

Exasperated at the slow progress Lady Butler-Sloss then challenged Mansfield to produce evidence to back the Fayed line that the deaths were murder not accidental.

Mansfield hit back with the unprecedented demand that the Queen be interviewed about claims by Diana's former butler Paul Burrell that Her Majesty had mentioned that "power's may be at work" over the Princess's death.

As the initial time estimate of a three month hearing with 40 witnesses doubled and then continued to spiral the plea by Diana's children for a "quick and transparent" inquiry seemed more and more distant.

Inquest into the Deaths of Diana,
Princess of Wales, and Dodi al-Fayed 2

Courtiers and coppers, spies and soothsayers, and lawyers and liars all gave evidence at the six-month inquest into the Paris car crash which killed the People's Princess. But the day Mohamed al-Fayed entered the witness box was unquestionably the most memorable.

It was the day he exposed himself not as a grieving father or victim of the Establishment, but a vindictive, foul-mouthed bully. He stepped forward clutching a seven-point statement prepared by his lawyers crystalising his case in sober terms, and pronounced "this is my moment." But within minutes the draft had gone out of the window and Fayed was into a full rant on his favourite theme of how the Duke of Edinburgh had ordered MI6 to kill Diana and his son.

Philip was a "racist and Nazi" and head of the family of "Draculas" who should be "sent back to Germany or from where he came from." "You want to know his original name," he went on. "It ends with Frankenstein ... well it sounds like Frankenstein. He is a person who grew up with the Nazis, brought up by auntie who married Hitler's general." He graciously omitted the Queen from his invective, but only because "I don't think she is as important as that."

But Prince Charles was a prime target. "He participated definitely because he would like to get on and marry his Camilla. This is what happened. They cleared the decks, they finished her (Diana), they murdered her and now he is happy.

"He married his crocodile wife and he is happy with that."

The 250-seat public gallery annexe in the High Court courtyard rocked with laughter – first at Fayed's colourful language and then at him. Here was a man not with a cogent case backed by evidence, but a bitter man who dedicated his life, reputation and multi-million pound fortune to a vendetta.

Everyone was against him, he said: The Royal Family, Diana's family, butler Paul Burrell, two Scotland Yard commissioners, secret service agents on both sides of the Channel and doctors, nurses and scientists in Paris and London. On top of that Fleet Street editors and reporters, politicians and, particularly, "stooge" judges were all part of the cover up.

"There seems to be an awful lot of people involved in this conspiracy," coroner Lord Justice Scott Baker noted drily.

In his summing up ten and a half years after the Princess's Mercedes had crashed head on into the reinforced concrete pillar in the Alma tunnel, the coroner told the jury there was "not a shred of evidence" to support Fayed's theory.

On 7 April 2008, having heard 250 witnesses over 94 days, they found the couple had been unlawfully killed. Not because of MI6 but through the gross negligence of the chasing paparazzi and Henri Paul, the Fayed employee who was allowed to drink before getting behind the wheel and then drove Diana and Dodi at twice the speed limit to their deaths.

R. *v* Nicholas van Hoogstraten

Nicholas van Hoogstraten revelled in his reputation as a really bad man.

The multi-millionaire rogue landlord treated his tenants, even those who paid his extortionate rents, and ramblers with a legal right to cross his land with the same contemptuous disregard.

After being in and out of jail in his early years when a judge said the tycoon believed himself to be "an emissary of Beelzebub", he started to consider himself untouchable.

But things started getting hot for him in July 1999 when a property rival Mohammed Raja was shot dead in front of his grandchildren in Sutton, Surrey.

At the Old Bailey in 2002 Robert Knapp and David Croke, who had links to Hoogstraten, were convicted of murder and sentenced to life imprisonment.

Hoogstraten was cleared of murder but found guilty of manslaughter and sentenced to 10 years and thousands in his old haunts of Brighton and Hove and West London breathed a mighty sigh of relief.

Mr Raja's son Amjad (pictured) had told the jury of Hoogstraten's threats and following the verdict went to the civil courts for compensation from him.

For years litigation dragged on with Hoogstaten being brought from prison and defending himself pouring abuse all over counsel and judges alike.

Matters became distinctly more serious when his manslaughter verdict was overturned by the Appeal Court and the familiar smirking figure dressed all in black walked free from the Old Bailey.

However the Raja family pressed on with their legal actions with heroic courage and perseverence and were rewarded in December 2005 when Hoogstraten was faced with having to pay them £6 million.

Mr Justice Lightman ruled, after hearing evidence which had been inadmissable at the original Old Bailey trial, that on the balance of probabilities, Hoogstraten had been responsible for recruiting henchmen Croke and Knapp to kill Mr Raja.

John Reid *v* Michael Flatley

He was worth £60 million and his feet alone, which famously could dance 28 taps a second, were insured for £25 million.

And when Michael Flatley was called to the witness box in court 60 at the High Court he warmed up as if he was going on stage.

Dressed in a blue suit, rather than his stage outfit of leather trousers vest and dancing shoes, Flatley rose to his feet then stretched his arms high above his head and shook them presumably to relieve tension in his shoulders.

The Irish-American star of *Riverdance* and *Lord of the Dance*, was defending himself in a £10 million breach of contract case brought by his former manager John Reid. Flatley counterclaimed alleging Reid had tricked him into signing an unfair contract.

The trial shone a cruel but highly entertaining light on the vanities and egocentricity of multi-million pound showbusiness stars.

Robert Englehart QC, representing Reid, told Mr Justice Lightman that Flatley had demanded he appear on more magazine covers, wanted to be nominated for the West End's Olivier Awards, wanted to appear in Hollywood films and wanted to be sponsored by the likes of Calvin Klein and Ralph Lauren.

Holidaying over Christmas 1996 in the Maldives, Flatley faxed his agent to express how "horribly disappointed" he had been that his management had not rung him with congratulations on reaching the top of the charts with a video of his show.

In the witness box Flatley said Reid had been so caught up with looking after his number one client Elton John, he had not had "enough time or interest to look after me."

He told how Reid, who had convictions for violence, had "abused and threatened" him in his dressing room before a show at Wembley, throwing faxes around, kicking a wastepaper basket and shouting and swearing.

Flatley was so upset after one outburst that he was physically ill.

But just as the metaphorical handbags were really being thrown around court, the case was settled on the eighth day of a trial due to last five weeks.

The dancer left court before the agreement was announced leaving Reid to tell reporters the allegations had been withdrawn and a "substantial payment" made to him.

The Hutton Inquiry into the death of Dr David Kelly

The death of Dr David Kelly, who was found dead in woods near his Oxfordshire home, shook the Government like little else in Tony Blair's 10 years in power.

Lord Hutton's remit was to "urgently conduct an investigation into the circumstances surrounding the death."

But while the tragic death was the focus of the inquiry, the constant backdrop was the infamous dossier on Iraq's alleged weapons of mass destruction and whether it had been "sexed up."

In August 2003 Blair became only the second serving Prime Minister to appear before a judicial inquiry set up by his own Government.

At 72 Lord Hutton was summoned from the Law Lords to court 73 of the High Court and he chose Oxford rugby blue James Dingemans QC as counsel to the inquiry.

For his day in court Blair was driven straight through to the yard where prisoners on appeal are usually unloaded and was met at a side door to be escorted upstairs.

Dozens of people had queued overnight outside court for the occasion and about 200 protestors made their views noisily plain in the Strand.

Suntanned from his recent holiday in Barbados, Blair was welcomed to the witness box by Mr Dingemans – who had asked everybody else giving evidence to formally state their name and job title – with the words: "I do not think we need an introduction."

Thereafter all the courtesies were observed on all sides with exchanges punctuated constantly with "prime minister" and "my lord."

For two hours and 20 minutes Blair emphasised that the central allegation that Downing Street had "sexed up" the dossier was so serious that, had it been true, he would have had to resign.

But other than that he kept at arm's length the nasty business of who knew what and when about Dr Kelly after the BBC report which caused the controversy and the tortuous ordeal of the weapons expert's final days.

For a politician who considered himself a "pretty straight kind of guy", Blair was cold, distant and very professional, but then his job was, potentially, on the line.

At the end of formal questioning Blair was asked if there was anything he wished to add about the circumstances of Dr Kelly's death. "No, I don't think there is," he replied rather too blithely.

Was there anything he'd care to say further? "No."

When Lord Hutton presented his report in January the next year the government survived comfortably while the BBC almost went into meltdown and very senior heads were to roll.

The Court of Appeal (Criminal Division):
Richard McIlkenny and others

On 14 March 1991 six men, by now mostly in late middle age, walked through the exit of the Old Bailey to an explosion of noise.

Crowds of reporters, sightseers and dozens from a local building site, had gathered as soon as the area had been closed and a TV microphone and stand placed in the middle of the road.

The Birmingham 6 had become the epitome of a miscarriage of justice in an era when the failings of the 1970s had to be corrected at an embarrassing frequent rate.

Over the preceeding days Graham Boal QC had made it clear in court the Crown no longer claimed the convictions were safe and satisfactory but all the evidence still had to be called to the satisfaction of Lord Justices Lloyd, Mustill and Farquharson before they would officially concur.

Like the Guildford 4, but unlike the Bridgewater 3, the appeal hearing was held at the Old Bailey and not its normal home at the Royal Courts of Justice.

In November 1974 twenty-one people had died in the bombing by the IRA of pubs in Birmingham city centtre.

The court heard how Richard McIlkenny, by now 57, Patrick Hill, 45, William Power, 44, John Walker, 55, Gerard Hunter, 42, and Hugh Callaghan, 60, were arrested in Heysham, Lancashire boarding a ferry to Belfast.

Disgracefully flawed forensic tests by Home Office scientist Dr Frank Skuse purported to have established that two, possibly three, of them had nitro-glycerine traces on their hands.

Confessions were beaten out of them and a number of police officers were named in court as having lied to secure convictions.

It took more than 10 years for Skuse's tests to be exposed as totally incompentent – soap would have produced the same results, according to Michael Mansfield QC.

He pointed out that justice pandered to the emotional outcry at this and other bombings on the mainland. There was just one month between the case being committed in May 1975 to the opening of the trial which was to end in the Six being jailed for life.

The original appeal was also controversially rejected by Lord Lane, the then Lord Chief Justice.

However, the Birmingham 6 case did play an important part in the creation of the Criminal Appeal Act of 1995 and the Criminal Case Review Commission in 1997.

Stephen Lawrence Inquiry
Norris questioned by
Michael Mansfield QC
Before
Lord Macpherson

Parents of
Stephen Lawrence
watch Michael Mansfield QC
with one of the
weapons

R. *v* Neil Acourt and others

Five men have been dragged before the criminal courts, a coroner's court and a public inquiry into the death of Stephen Lawrence.

They have even had their faces splashed across the front page of a national newspaper as the killers of the 18-year-old student.

For 14 years the smug and defiant suspects, Neil and Jamie Acourt, Gary Dobson, Luke Knight and David Norris, have denied any part in the murder.

But nothing matched the drama of Michael Mansfield QC producing a weapon in court during cross examination in an attempt to shock them out of their complacency of denial and alleged forgetfulness with which they consistently evaded questioning.

It was a stunning moment in more than a decade of court hearings and police investigations which have brought little but renewed despair for Neville and Doreen Lawrence.

Their son had been stabbed to death by a gang of white youths in a blatantly racist attack at a bus stop in Eltham in April 1993.

The murder inquiry floundered almost immediately sparking allegations of neglect of duty, incompetence and even corruption.

Frustrated, the Lawrences launched a private prosecution which ended with Neil Acourt, Dobson and Knight being sent for trial at the Old Bailey and charges against Norris and Jamie Acourt being thrown out at a magistrates court for lack of evidence.

In April 1996 the Old Bailey trial also ended prematurely in the middle of the prosecution case with the suspects being formally aquitted.

A few months later and Mansfield gets to question them for the first time at Southwark Coroners Court, when they cynically parrot "I can't remember" answers.

The furious coroner Sir Montague Levine is powerless to do more than record a verdict of "unlawful killing." The *Daily Mail* prints the suspects' pictures with the headline "Murderers."

In 1997 Home Secretary, Jack Straw, announced an inquiry to be led by 72-year-old Sir William Macpherson of Cluny. When the hearing opens the following year the suspects are ordered to give evidence, but again give nothing away.

In a clear sign of pent up aggression they lash out under a torrent of abuse and missiles showered on them by the crowd gathered to see them leave the inquiry centre in the Elephant and Castle.

In a controversial report Macpherson concludes the Met police are unwittingly insitutionally racist.

New police investigations are launched but no-one is charged. In a final sad chapter in 1999 Stephen's parents divorce after 28 years.

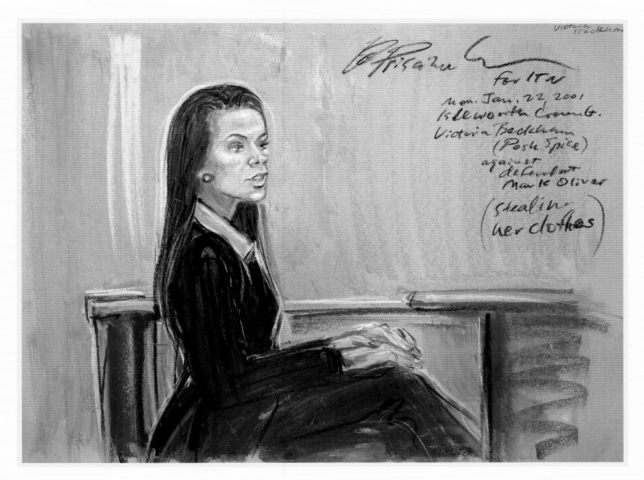

R. *v* Mark Oliver

Isleworth Crown Court is not a pretty place. Nestling in the suburbs of the less nice parts of Hounslow it is a long, long way from Knightsbridge and Rodeo Drive. So imagine the distaste of Mrs Victoria Beckham as she picked her way past the flotsam and jetsam of West London's underworld who frequent the corridors of the capital's least prestigious court building on a Monday morning in January 2001.

She was on her way to give evidence in the trial of an unemployed binman accused of stealing her Louis Vuitton luggage as she passed through Heathrow airport on her way home from holiday in Miami.

At that time husband David was captain of England and still a Manchester United hero, while she was positively post-Posh Spice and had her eyes firmly trained on the late Princess Diana's role of fashion icon of the world.

An extremely limited number of press tickets were issued two hours before she arrived at court in a chauffeur driven Mercedes with blacked out windows, and the public had even less access to the tiny courtroom.

Once installed in the witness box and dressed in a tight-fitting dark outfit over beige blouse, she told how "near enough all my clothes" and "priceless" items, such as love messages from David and a lock of son Brooklyn's hair, had gone missing.

Defendant Mark Oliver, 20, had actually contacted the star – through her nail technician, the court was told – offering to return some of her possessions he had allegedly found.

He told her that her clothing and personal treasures had been dumped in binliners in his truck behind his back. He returned some of her Spice Girls' lyrics and a silver-framed photograph of husband and eldest son given to her as a Valentine present.

When the police paid Oliver a visit they found more than £1,000-worth of designer clothes in his sister's wardrobe.

Little more than 24 hours after her evidence Oliver, a convicted thief with a record of violence, was found guilty of two charges of handling stolen goods. He was jailed for 15 months.

Most of the contents of Mrs Beckham's luggage was never recovered and British Airways paid her £100,000 in compensation.

However the style princess was given the benefit of DC Andre Lucker's expert advice: "Although Louis Vuitton won't thank me for saying so, all passengers should travel with sturdy, secure and anonymous luggage."

R. *v* Michael Stone

Lin Russell was walking home from school with her two daughters aged six and nine through fields in the heart of the Garden of England.

Only one of them survived as mother, youngest daughter and even their pet dog Lucy were battered to death with a sledge hammer.

The appalling crime was immediately linked in the nation's mind with the name of the sole and miraculous survivor – Josie Russell.

Two years later in October 1998 Michael Stone, a mentally deranged heroin addict with a history of violence, was convicted and sentenced to three life sentences at Maidstone Crown Court.

But controversy has always surrounded the case, which was based not on forensic evidence but the testimony of convicted prisoners banged up with Stone before his trial.

Astonishingly in such a blood bath the killer left no evidence of himself at the murder scene in Cherry Garden Lane, near Chillenden, Kent.

But a large number of prisoners came forward to say that Stone had confessed to them, and even bragged about smashing the victims' heads like eggshells and tying them up with wet towels – the children had been attending a swimming gala.

After the guilty verdicts one of the prisoners, Barry Thompson, claimed he had lied and, as a substantial miscarriage of justice campaign gathered momentum, a retrial was ordered by the Appeal Court (above).

At the second trial at Nottingham Crown Court in October 2001 Stone was convicted again by a 10–2 majority. Nigel Sweeney QC had replaced Anne Rafferty QC for the prosecution but William Clegg QC remained defence counsel.

In each trial Josie's remarkable evidence, carefully teased out by brilliant liaison officers over the months following her life-saving surgery, was played to the jury in a video compilation.

But the key figure was former prisoner Damien Daley who, at both Maidstone and Nottingham, told how Stone had boasted about the murders through a cracked pipe linking their cells in the segregation wing of Canterbury prison.

As he left court on each occassion Daley fixed Stone with the most fearsome stare. It chilled everyone present let alone the man in his sights sitting in the dock.

R. *v* Kevin Maxwell and others

Three years and six months after Robert Maxwell was found floating in the Atlantic his two sons went on trial charged with using shares belonging to *Daily Mirror* pensioners to prop up the tycoon's ailing companies.

The outcry against the heavyweight multimillionaire was such that when Alan Suckling QC opened the case in May 1995 at Chichester Rents in Chancery Lane, few people in the country believed that Kevin and Ian Maxwell had not known what their father had been up to.

Yet at the end of the six-month trial the brilliant defence masterminded by Alun Jones QC and Clare Montgomery QC led the jury to acquit the brothers, and their late father's former aides Larry Trachtenberg and Robert Bunn, on all charges.

Kevin Maxwell alone gave evidence for 70 hours over 21 days and the jury took seven days to return unanimous verdicts, which at that time was almost a record.

But this was not the end of the matter as the Serious Fraud Office insisted Kevin Maxwell should still face a second trial on fresh charges, with the possibility of a third at some time in the future.

When Maxwell went to the High Court to apply for a stay on proceedings, he was astonished to see three jurors from the trial had turned up for the legal argument to show their support for him.

But the clinching argument came from Pandora, Maxwell's wife and mother of their six children. In an impassioned plea she described the agony of the trial and how her children had been taunted in the playground that their father was going to prison.

Halting the prosecution Mr Justice Buckley paid the most handsome judicial tribute to a wife since the "elegant, fragrant and radiant" description of Mary Archer nine years earlier.

"Her obvious distress was, I am convinced, entirely genuine," said the judge, "No-one could have been unmoved by her evidence."

He went on to point out that the Maxwell investigation had already cost the taxpayer at least £20 million and to pursue lesser charges after the original not guilty verdicts could hardly be in the public interest.

Maxwell held a press conference in Lincoln's Inn where he praised his wife and added: "It's still my view that my father was not dishonest and that he did not commit suicide. It was an accident."

As a result of the failed prosecution the SFO came in for heavy criticism and there were new calls for non-jury trials in complex fraud cases – a debate which still rages more than a decade later.

High Court (Family Division): Miss B

From a NHS hospital bed somewhere in South East England a woman paralysed from the neck down told a judge in a clear but anguished voice: "I want to be able to die."

In March 2002 Dame Elizabeth Butler-Sloss, lawyers and court staff joined medics around the bedside in an *ad hoc* courtroom to hear this extraordinary evidence.

The whole operation was relayed via a TV link back to the High Court where, later that day, the hearing reopened in the more normal surroundings.

The right-to-die case was brought by Miss B, a 43-year-old former social-care professional who had been paralysed 11 months earlier by a burst blood vessel.

Through her lawyers she argued that her quality of life was now unbearable and she wanted the right to have her life support machine turned off.

Her application was opposed by the hospital doctors, and, not for the first or last time, Dame Elizabeth was left to make a monumentally delicate human as well as legal judgement.

"Whatever the outcome of this case it has been a pleasure to meet you," the judge told the brave and impressively honest woman.

A court official held the Bible to Miss B's right hand as a ventilator pumped air over her vocal cords so she could talk and breathe.

Her counsel Philip Havers QC asked if it was her wish to be allowed to leave the hospital and be taken to another medical centre where the doctors were willing to switch of her life support machine.

"Yes," she replied.

Robert Francis QC, representing the NHS trust running the hospital, asked: "Is it your wish to die or is it your wish not to remain alive in your present condition?"

"The latter," she replied.

Dame Elizabeth pointed out to Miss B that she had chosen a very difficult and still evolving section of the law. "You have raised an issue most people would wish to avoid."

After 70-minutes the judge and counsel were driven back to the High Court and the continued legal argument which was to last another week was relayed back by TV to Miss B's bedside.

In a reserved judgment Dame Elizabeth ruled that Miss B did have the mental capacity to refuse treatment and within a few days she was moved to a new hospital where her wishes were carried out.

R. v A, B

More than a decade on, what happened in Bootle shopping centre and on the long march over one and a half miles to the murder scene at the railway tracks is still utterly chilling.

When the body of two-year-old James Bulger was found, Robert Thompson and Jon Venables, then aged 10 were picked up quickly and, eventually, came to tell what occured.

At Preston Crown Court the wave of fury sweeping the country was well hidden. No angry mobs behind police cordons, the locals seemed more interested in the UK snooker championships running simultaneously at the Guildhall opposite.

Inside the dark courtroom the glowering presence of the Bulger family, led by mother Denise, sat on the left and the parents of the two boys were on the right. They were fretful, nervous, occassionally tearful, not wanting to be seen ever to smile.

In the dock the tiny defendants sat between social workers on raised seats.

For the defence David Turner QC and Brian Walsh QC had limited options.

Once the old canard of prejudicial press reporting had failed, they turned to the question of whether the boys were too young to know the difference between right and wrong. The school head teacher put an end to that.

Prosecutor Richard Henriques QC's main job was to keep a lid on the heat.

Those present felt almost under a duty to hold their breath.

When the jury was out Mr Justice Moreland ruled that the defendants (up until then known in the press as boy A and Boy B) could be named on a guilty verdict.

At the time it seemed the right decision but it has since been criticised and anonymity of their new identities has been reimposed for their safety after release.

Sweeping changes to the way juveniles are tried for serious crimes have also been introduced.

The guilty verdicts were inevitable and as the small murderers were driven away it felt as if a cork had been blown out of the bottle as a screaming mob surrounded the courthouse.

R. *v* Ian Huntley, Maxine Carr

From the Moors murderers to Madeline McCann nothing grips the public like a child abduction and killing.

Once Holly Wells and Jessica Chapman, the two pretty young girls in Manchester United shirts, had disappeared in the heat of August 2003 in Soham, Cambridgeshire and all the way to number one court at the Old Bailey in December, the public demand for news – any news – never slackened.

Even weeks into proccedings the trial of Ian Huntley and Maxine Carr led TV bulletins and newspapers – the *Evening Standard* alone splashed it on its front page on 18 days and devoted 76 pages in all to the case.

All of which put immense pressure on counsel and Mr Justice Moses.

Richard Latham QC's calm, authorative style was perfectly suited to presenting the Crown's case. He had overwhelming evidence against Huntley, but Carr, who was charged with lying for her boyfriend, was different.

Carefully led by Michael Hubbard QC, she burned with a sense of injustice, distancing herself from Huntley and any notion that she had known he had lured the girls to his house, killed them, and burned and dumped their bodies miles away.

"I'm not going to be blamed for what THAT thing in that box has done to me or those children," she yelled from the witness box across the courtroom.

The moment when Carr denounced her former live-in lover was the most electrifying moment of an electrifying trial.

For Stephen Coward QC it was a hopeless case. Huntley was illogical, tearful and self-pitying in the witness box.

The jury was out for three days, no doubt uncertain over Carr's role. In the end Huntley was jailed for life and Carr was sentenced to three and a half years for perverting the course of justice.

R. *v* Paul Burrell

On a Friday morning in November 2002 Paul Burrell walked free from the Old Bailey number one court rejoicing that "the Lady's pulled through for me."

The butler's trial for allegedly stealing from his "boss", Diana, Princess of Wales, treasured family gifts and her most intimate letters and photographs had run for three weeks but barely sat in front of the jury for more than a handful of days.

Burrell's fate was decided not in the jury room but behind the scenes in Mrs Justice Rafferty's chambers, CPS headquarters in Ludgate Hill and Buckingham Palace.

As a result the case was dropped on the eve of Burrell entering the witness box armed with his encyclopaedic knowledge of Diana's secrets and the potentially embarrassing inner workings of the Queen's household.

The crux came when the Queen – en route to the Bali bomb victims memorial service at St Paul's – remembered Burrell had mentioned keeping some of Diana's letters for safe keeping.

The police and CPS were informed of Her Majesty's timely recollection and the climbdown process was put into operation.

The trial had opened with a frenzy of anticipation with TV cameramen from US TV stations and press from across Europe, Asia and Australia.

Burrell, every inch the gentleman's gentleman in a well cut suit and expensive shirt, shoes, tie and cufflinks, was outwardly cool but white-faced with worry.

The police had raided his home in Cheshire and seized a treasure trove of Diana and her sons' possessions which would have fetched millions in any sale.

They included dozens of dresses, jewellry, signed letters and family photographs. Some, like the baby Prince Harry in the bath, were so personal they had to be passed around court under a cover, away from the eyes of the press shoe-horned out of the way at the back of court.

Burrell had told police he had taken them for safe keeping and had the permission of the Princess before her death or from members of her family.

Some of the evidence was sensational – the police had allegedly told Prince Charles that Burrell had been photogrphed wearing Diana's dresses. Some witnesses, particularly Diana's mother and sister, spoke of the sadness of family rows with the Princess that were unable to be resolved before it was too late.

But after William Boyce QC had opened the case and called just a few witnesses it was all over and the charges were dropped.

A month later the trial of a second butler, Harold Brown employed by Diana and Princess Margaret, who was facing similar charges collapsed before it had even started.

Jeffrey Archer *v* Express Newspapers

There was something wrong but nobody could put their finger on it.

Jeffrey Archer – as he then was – the multi-millionaire novelist and ex-deputy Conservative party chairman was in a hole and knew it.

Sweating and straining he stood in the witness box insisting he could not have had sex with prostitute Monica Coghlan.

Nobody suspected then that the diary he held in his hand to substantiate his alibi was a complete hoax.

The *Daily Star*, following up a *News of the World* exclusive, claimed he had met Miss Coghlan in Shepherd's Market, Mayfair and taken her to a hotel in Victoria. The *Sunday* newspaper even provided photos of Archer's go-between paying her £1,000 to go away at Victoria station.

Archer sued for libel and so there he was in court 13 of the High Court being desperately unconvincing but, lacking the vital evidence, George Hill QC, for the *Star*, could not quite nail him.

But once he was out of the witness box and the immaculately-dressed, loftily disdainful but ever loyal Mary Archer went in, the whole case changed.

Mr Justice Caulfield simpy fell in love with her. "She is a vision you will never forget. Has she elegance? Has she fragrance? Would she have, without the strain of this trial, a radiance?" he told the jury in his now notorious summing up.

Why would any man married to such a woman prefer "cold, unloving, rubber-insulated sex in a seedy hotel" with a common prostitute?

Robert, later Lord, Alexander QC simply ripped into poor Monica (pictured), reducing her – and the *Star*'s case – to a blubbering wreck. Humiliated and shaking with waves of tears she asked for a hankie, and the judge contemptuously backhanded a box of Kleenex at her.

Archer won £500,000 and bounced back into the affections of the Tory party.

More importantly he considered himself bulletproof – nobody would dare challenge him now.

R. *v* Lord Archer

So now we know. In tabloid terms it was "the diary what won it."

Not only had Archer, now made Lord Archer by a grateful party leader, tried to rope an old friend into lying for him about the night of the alleged liaison with Monica Coghlan, but the diary was a sham.

Fourteen years later, Archer was back in court but this time it was court eight at the Old Bailey and this time the judge was never going to fall for the charms of his apparently long-suffering wife.

This time it was Mr Justice Potts and things were going to be very different.

Archer was charged with perjury and perverting the course of justice at the 1987 libel trial.

Co-defendant Ted Francis had actually blown the whistle on his former friend by admitting Archer had asked him to provide a false alibi, even though it was not in the end used against the Daily Star.

But the key witness was former secretary Angela Peppiatt (pictured), who revealed not only the truth about the diary but also – reluctantly – what Fleet Street had long known but never dared to print – that Archer was incapable of fidelity to his wife and had innumerable affairs.

Lady Archer still stood by her man for the cameras. Arriving ostentatiously each day at the front door of court she walked straight through to be picked up out of sight by her chauffeur at the back door.

When she came to give evidence the haughty superiority just didn't work. Instead of the reverence she expected she was mocked by David Waters QC who first teased her then exposed the holes and false assumptions in her evidence.

It was not what the Archers were used to and they were further incensed when the judge did not immediately allow him to leave the dock to attend his dying mother. "She's 87," Lady Archer yelled across court.

Nicholas Purnell QC's closing speech spanned two days but the evidence against Archer was overwhelming and he was jailed for four years. Francis was acquitted of one charge of intent to pervert the course of justice by helping Archer.

Polanski *v Vanity Fair*

Oscar-winning film director Roman Polanski had to go to the House of Lords to enable him to win £50,000 damages from *Vanity Fair*.

The premier libel trial of 2005 was not just a landmark case it positively groaned with irony.

The Law Lords allowed the director of *Chinatown* and *The Pianist* while he was on the run from the law to sue an American magazine in a British court while never setting foot outside France.

To give evidence his face appeared on TV screens around court 13 of the High Court while he sat in a suite of the George V hotel in Paris.

Had he hopped on a Eurostar train and turned up in court in person he would have run the risk of arrest and extradition to the US where in 1977 he had pleaded guilty to having sex with a 13-year-old girl before fleeing from justice.

By a 3/2 majority the highest court in England decided that even a fugitive who admitted a serious crime was entitled to have his civil liberties protected by the courts.

So it was that Polanski, now 72, via the video link told John Kelsey-Fry QC and the jury of the anguish caused by the magazine's allegations of a strange occasion 33 years previously.

It had claimed Polanski had run his hand up the leg of an aspiring actress in Elaine's restaurant in New York and offered to make her "the new Sharon Tate."

This incident was said to have happened when he was on his way to Los Angeles for the funeral of Sharon Tate, his first wife who had been murdered by Charles Manson.

Mia Farrow (pictured), star of Polanski's *Rosemary's Baby*, had been present that night and told the court the incident never happened.

While the mystery actress, who turned out to be Norweigan Beatte Telle, never came to court at all.

Tom Shields QC said Polanski's self-confessed perversion and renegade status meant he had no reputation in this country to lose.

But the jury decided the incident had never taken place and the director had been maligned.

"Outrageous," was *Vanity Fair* editor Grayson Carter's reaction.

R. *v* Rosemary West

Plump, middle aged, bespectacled housewives are not normally serial killers.

But Rosemary West was unique in many ways. Egged on by her perverted husband Fred, the mother-of-ten happily turned herself into a receptacle for sex and presided over mass murder.

When he tired of her body she helped recruit younger, unwitting replacements, including her own children and if they proved obstinate unwilling or even disrespectful to his needs, she watched as he destroyed then buried the evidence.

The House of Horrors trial – the judge actually banned the expression – contained the most gruesome evidence imaginable.

When it was first heard – read by prosecutor Neil Butterfield QC at the committal at Dursley, Gloucestershire – even the gallows humour of Fleet Street's most experienced hacks was silenced.

By that time Fred had hung himself in prison and Rose entered the dock at Winchester Crown Court alone in October 1995 to face ten murder charges.

The Dursley prosecutor had become Mr Justice Butterfield, so Brian Leveson QC faced Richard Ferguson QC and Sasha Wass.

Levenson had his hands full. Some of the murders dated back years, others relied on the random memories of neighbours and some victims were girls with few friends, family or ties and who simply disappeared.

But there was telling evidence of how Rose went out driving with Fred – just like Ian Brady and Myra Hindley – to pick up young victims lured by the reassuring presence in the car of the mumsy housewife. Once back at their Gloucester home the couple subjected the victims to sexual torture and a grave in the garden.

As the evidence unfolded Rose blinked benignly from the dock.

At one stage a tape of a police interview was played to the court with Fred's own thick West Country voice revelling in his evil.

Silence in court is an old cliché, but this was compelling. No one dared move. Truly the only sound was of jurors simultaneously turning the pages of their transcripts.

After two days' deliberations the jury returned ten guilty verdicts and as the clock jerked towards 1 p.m., Mr Justice Mantell uttered the words heard by only a handful of murderers:

"You will never be released."

R. *v* Barry George

Was this case a true miscarriage of justice or was the dysfunctional loner Barry George the right and only man who could have shot dead Jill Dando?

The BBC presenter was so popular many people can still remember where they were when they heard she had been killed, just like other icons Kennedy, Diana and Lennon.

It took the police 12 months to arrest George and when the case came to court one of the Old Bailey they knew there was a shortage of hard evidence.

Orlando Pownall QC, prosecuting, painted a picture of the killer as a troubled fantasist who liked guns, lived near Dando's home, once worked at the BBC and occupied a make believe world of celebrity worship.

He was in or around Gowan Avenue, Fulham when Dando was shot on her doorstep and repeatedly lied to the police.

But if it wasn't George who was it?

The killing may have held all the hallmarks of a professional job, but who would want to take a contract out on Jill Dando? A disgruntled crime boss brought down by the *Crimewatch* programme she fronted?

Michael Mansfield QC hinted, and was much mocked by Mr Pownall, that Serbian warlords might have been angered by her appearance on TV appealing for aid for Kosovan refugees.

As the arguments raged George could not cope and a nurse was summoned to hold his hand to keep his pulse down and panic attacks under control.

The crucial evidence was the disputed microscopic speck of gunpowder found in a pocket of George's coat.

It was all that was gleaned from a search of his entire home. Was it the true link to Jill Dando's murder or was it contamination or just a red herring caused by contact with others?

George was found guilty in 2001 and sentenced to life imprisonment. In November 2007 the Appeal Court ruled that the speck of gunpowder could no longer be said to prove anything at all and that a fresh jury would have to decide George's fate.

R. *v* Barry George 2

Nine years after Jill Dando was shot in the back of her head on her own doorstep, Barry George returned to the dock of court one at the Old Bailey.

Nine years had passed since her shocking death and seven years since George's first trial, but so much had changed.

George himself still looked dopey and dim witted but he was also much sharper and more confident. He didn't blink around the court in confusion, he knew where he was, he knew what was going on and what he wanted and he sent orders to his legal team.

Miss Dando herself was a more distant memory. Her warmth, her beauty, her sunniness, which was so vivid at the time of the first trial had, inevitably, faded. There was now half a generation of people who had grown up never having seen her on TV. Extraordinarily, thanks to the fight to prove his innocence, George was now a better known name than the 1990s TV personality.

There was change of personnel at the Bar too. Jonathan Laidlaw QC led for the Crown and William Clegg QC had been drafted in at short notice before the appeal which had led to the retrial.

In terms of evidence the prosecution had lost the invisible speck of firearms discharge found in a a coat pocket in George's home, which the Appeal Court had ruled worthless. But they had gained the now admissable bad character evidence of George's appetite for stalking women.

However they were not allowed to tell the jury of George's previous convictions for sexual violence – nor his arrest in the grounds of Kensington Palace in full combat gear allegedly in pursuit of Princess Diana.

The defence stepped back from the faintly ridiculous theory that a Serbian warlord had ordered the killing and relied on the prosecution being unable to prove its case.

Once again George, who was allowed to sit next to clinical pscych-ologist Dr Susan Young throughout the trial, was ruled to be medically unfit to give evidence.

Mr Justice Griffith Williams told the jury fair and square that if they believed that the handful of witnesses called to prove that George had been in Miss Dando's street, Gowan Avenue, Fulham, on the day of the shooting were mistaken – and only one had positively identified George in a police line up – then they must acquit immediately. In the 14 hours of deliberations the three notes the jurors sent to the judge showed that this was the crucial area.

The not guilty verdict was unanimous.

George looked stunned and turned to go down to the cells for the last time. His sister Michelle Diskin who had led his freedom campaign yelled and punched the air. George was now officially a victim of a miscarriage of justice, but no one was any nearer knowing who had killed Jill Dando.

Neil Hamilton *v* Mohamed al-Fayed, the *Guardian*

The libel trial Neil Hamilton *v* Mohamed al-Fayed was really, as the *Sun* put it, "Liar *v* Liar."

Hamilton, the Tory MP for Tatton, summed up everything the public despised about sleaze and the dying days of 18 years of Conservative government.

Fayed, owner of Harrods, was renown for his outrageous comments which had forced him to pay out in a string of libel cases settled out of court.

The issue was: Did Hamilton accept £30,000 from Fayed, as alleged in the *Guardian*, for asking questions for him in the Commons?

By the time the case came to court Hamilton, backed by "well wishers"money, was an ex-MP.

His counsel Desmond Browne QC gambled by allowing the defence to open first, hoping Fayed would crumble in the witness box and settle.

In fact Fayed started well. "You can call me Al Capone," he told Browne to laughter, but was soon tempted to head off on his Prince Philip killed Diana theories.

Although Mr Justice Moreland was to tell the jury in his summing up to ignore everything Fayed said unless it was supported by other evidence, the Harrods boss emerged reasonably unscathed from cross examination.

Not so the Hamiltons. Three times George Carman QC recited the long bar bill they ran up, at Fayed's expense, at the Ritz in Paris.

"On the make and on the take," became Carman's mantra.

Plus Carman had another ace, Peter Whiteman QC, a former advisor to Mobil, who told how Hamilton had asked him for money to table a Commons amendment favourable to the oil giant.

This was the crucial back up evidence for Fayed and when the jury returned their verdict Hamilton threw his head in hands in despair.

Since then he spent more of his supporters' money on a failed appeal and went bankrupt in failing to meet the *Guardian*'s costs.

But like bad pennies Neil and Christine keep on turning up, usually on TV where they seem cheerful enough.

Ian Botham and Allan Lamb *v* Imran Khan

They were giants on the cricket field and totems of their very different cultures.

In 1996 Ian Botham was the hero of Anglo-Saxon muscularity. The hard drinking slayer of the Aussies was everything the lager-swilling, *Eng-er-lund* chanting sports fan aspired to be.

Eleven years before his knighthood he was very much a rebel.

Imran Khan was Oxford-educated, Muslim, devotional, teetotal, and serious-minded. On the field his leadership of Pakistan had taken a talented but ragged group of individuals to World Cup victory and brought pride to a nation at home and a community in Britain.

It wasn't Lords but court 13 at the High Court yet the animostiy between the two from their cricket clashes was palpable.

What is more the case provided another round in the rivalry between George Carman QC, representing Imran, and Charles Gray QC, for Botham.

Botham and his friend, England batsman Allan Lamb, had sued Imran for libel over an alleged interview in a magazine which was said to have accused them of ball tampering, racism and being low class.

Imran, who came to court with his fey and unfeasibly gorgeous wife Jemima, denied making the allegations.

But from the opening over Botham, accompanied by his down-to-earth wife Kathy, laced into his rival.

Clearly seething in the witness box Botham fixed him with a fearsome glare at a range of barely a few feet, and, with ice in his words, told him: "I would like to inform Imran that my wife and I have a very successful marriage, thank you."

A parade of past and present cricket stars passed through the witness box to give their tuppence worth about ball tampering, including Geoff Boycott, who was unwittingly hilarious, and David Gower who swung the case Imran's way by elegantly shrugging aside some of the alleged slurs he said could equally have applied to him.

The verdict was a surprise to those who expected an English jury would side only with the country's great sporting hero.

Botham took it badly and was determined to appeal but eventually abandoned hope. Now of course he is a grandfather and knight of the realm.

Imran is still venerated and built a major cancer hospital in memory of his mother. But he failed to achieve his ultimate political goal and, ironically, it was his marriage which was to fail.

R. *v* Ricky Preddie, Danny Preddie

The Damilola Taylor murder case swung from being the most disspiriting trial I have ever seen to a final and belated triumph.

Across three trials marred by shambolic errors, frustrations and confusion, the one point of constancy was the presence of Richard and Gloria Taylor.

Quiet and dignified, they betrayed little of the bitter frustration or anger they understandably felt at the blunders in evidence and investigation which piled up week after week.

In the end they were rewarded with verdicts of manslaughter against two of the seven young thugs charged with the murder of their 10-year-old son.

As these verdicts were returned Ricky Preddie, 19, and his 18-year-old brother Danny suddenly burst into screaming and swearing at jurors, the police, and the judge and had to be bundled out of court and down to the cells.

Damilola, a happy, pleasant if not terribly gifted boy, had been skipping home from school in November 2000 when he was set upon by a gang of teenagers in Peckham.

He was stabbed in the leg with a broken beer bottle – quite possibly for not handing over the distinctive silver puffa jacket he was wearing – and collapsed bleeding to death in a stairwell of a block of flats.

Four youths were originally charged with murder but the 2002 trial turned into a fiasco with the main prosecution witness, a girl known as Bromley, being stripped of all credibility in cross examination, particularly by Courtenay Griffiths QC and Lady Mallalieu QC.

But from the wreckage of this trial a new police investigation started and fresh forensic evidence of previously missed blood stains led to new arrests.

Four years later in 2006 three new suspects, including the Preddie brothers, were charged and cleared of murder. But the jury was unable to agree a verdict on the alternative manslaughter charges.

The Crown Prosecution Service bravely went for a third trial which ended with the guilty verdicts on the brothers, who were just 12 and 13 at the time of Damilola's violent death.

Mr Justice Goldring sentenced them to eight years.

R. *v* Tony Martin

Was Tony Martin a hero or a dangerous killer or just mentally unstable?

The Norfolk farmer shot dead a 16-year-old boy fleeing from his house in an attempted burglary.

Had the victim been the lad's older accomplice, mentor and career thief Brendan Fearon instead would there have been an outcry let alone a conviction at all?

Fearon and teenager Fred Barras had driven 70 miles from Newark to break into Martin's isolated farm, the aptly-named Bleak House in Emmeth Hungate.

Martin shot Fearon in the legs but Barrras was running away when he was struck in the back and left to die in the garden.

The trial, held in one of the smaller most claustrophobic courts at Norwich Crown Court in 2000, fizzed with tension, resentment, and allegations of jury nobbling.

Martin was backed by a tidal wave of public support who believed an Englishman had a right to defend his castle, particularly when it had been repeatedly targeted by burglars.

But the travelling community turned up in strength to support their own.

The police were also out in force equipped with CS spray and batons, which was ironic considering the chief constable had admitted he could not provide sufficient cover to deter crime at remote rural homes.

Martin, a bewildered figure throughout the trial, pleaded not guilty to murder but his muddled account of the shooting was exposed by the ballistic evidence.

He was cleared of attempting to murder Fearon but found guilty of murdering Barras by a 10 to 2 majority and sentenced to life.

However the conviction was overturned on appeal and a five-year sentence substituted for manslaughter on the grounds of diminished responsibility.

Now defended by Michael Wolkind QC, the court heard that credible evidence had since emerged that Martin had been suffering from a paranoid personality disorder at the time of the killing.

The farmer had refused to be examined by a psychiatrist before the trial so that his legal team, then led by Anthony Scrivenor QC, had been unable to run a mental health defence.

Fearon, who had been jailed for three years for the break-in, continued to steal and has had several more prison sentences. Ever the snide chancer, he tried to sue for compensation for his injuries – unsuccessfully.

R. *v* David Copeland

Mad or bad? Can juries really find the truth inside the twisted mind of a serial killer?

David Copeland, known as the Nazi Nailbomber, was convicted of murder but, like the Yorkshire Ripper Peter Sutcliffe, he ended up not in prison but Broadmoor maximum security hospital.

What is undeniable is that the verdicts did bring comfort to the injured survivors, including Gary Reid who attended every day of his trial in a wheelchair.

Copeland, 24, killed three people and injured 139 in three bombings across London around Easter 1999 in Brick Lane, Brixton and the Admiral Duncan pub in Soho.

Each bomb, packed with nails for maximum destruction, death and maiming, was motivated by hatred – either racial or homophobic.

The victims were ordinary passers-by in the street, market traders and West End theatre-goers enjoying a drink before the show.

Having hung around the fringes of extreme right wing politics, Copeland felt inspired by the scenes of panic, death and injuries caused by the Atlanta Olympics bomb in 1996 to reach out for his goal of becoming a famous mass murderer.

When he was finally arrested at his parents' home in Yateley, Hampshire he told police: "Yeah, they are all down to me, I did them on my own" and spoke of further plans to strike in Southall, Tottenham and Peckham.

At the Old Bailey, Michael Wolkind QC argued that Copeland was mentally disturbed at the time of the bombings and so guilty of only manslaughter on the grounds of diminished responsibility.

A succession of psychiatrists debated the extent of his delusions and psychopathic paranoia.

The jury found him guilty of three charges of murder and three counts of causing an explosion. The Recorder of London Michael Hyam QC sentenced him to six life sentences.

The doctors did agree that his mental state since his arrest had deteriorated so markedly he should be sent not to Belmarsh prison but straight to Broadmoor.

Copeland was not happy. "Not Broadmoor," he told a doctor. "It's a living death, 100 times worse than Belmarsh."

McCartney *v* Mills-McCartney

Whenever Paul McCartney's tunes are hummed people will remember his ex-wife tipped a jug of water over his divorce lawyer in court.

Fiona Shackleton was known as the Steel Magnolia not only for her hard as hell negotiating stance but also her stately hairdo. Looking suspiciously sustained by a blizzard of hairspray, it presents an impressive even intimidating edifice on top of her six-foot plus height in high heels.

On the day the divorce deal was announced in March 2008 she strode into court shoulder to shoulder with her client. Two hours later, as the nation's press surrounded Heather Mills as she delivered an extraordinary attack on justice on the High Court steps, Miss Shackleton slipped out virtually unnoticed thoroughly drenched. Only Priscilla Coleman detected what had happened in the closed court session and set to work with her crayons.

Weeks later Miss Mills would proudly claim that she had overheard some muttered remark by her nemesis and decided to "cleanse and baptise her." Ironically the wet look transformed the lawyer's image. One newspaper compared her normal stern-faced bouffant look to Camilla, Duchess of Cornwall and her sleeked-back smiling visage to Diana, Princess of Wales.

The water gag was a fascinating insight into the showbiz celebrity divorce battle of the decade and the demons driving Miss Mills. She originally wanted £125 million out of what she claimed was his £800 million fortune. Increasingly frustrated that she could not even prove her estimate of his wealth – the judge placed it at £400 million – she railed against Sir Paul, the judge and, needless to say, Miss Shackleton and ended up having to represent herself in court.

Finally she had to accept a £24.3 million settlement and then failed to prevent the scathing judgement of Mr Justice Bennett being made public. He described her as "devoid of reality", "a less than candid witness", "her own worst enemy" and "quite inconsistent" in pages and pages of unflattering comment. The nation loved it.

McCartney, as a former Beatle with the chirpy, ever-youthful face previously married to the equally saintly, vegetarian Linda, could do no wrong. Mills, 15 years his junior, was dismissed as nothing more than a gold digger. Rightly or wrongly the media-fuelled stereotyping was set and there was nothing she could say or do to change the popular perception encapsulated in the case's nickname: Macca *v* Mucca.

R. *v* Jane Andrews

Hollywood loves a femme fatale, a woman who is irresistible to men but leads them through love and passion to tragedy.

Jane Andrews was more of a fatal woman who killed her lover Tommy Cressman through cynical, cold blooded anger because he didn't want to marry her. In the middle of the night she hit him over the head with a cricket bat as he slept then plunged a knife through his heart right up to the hilt.

Having rigged the murder scene at their Fulham home to look as if she had had to beat off his own violent sexual attack on her, she drove down to the West Country to concoct a suitable defence.

Andrews had been the Duchess of York's dresser and had helped her run up mountainous debts in shopping malls across Britain, Europe and the United States. Although Grimsby-born, she had met Cressman, the son of a multi-millionaire American car dealer, on a blind date in Beauchamp Place, Knightsbridge in 1998 and decided his was the lifestyle she wanted to become accustomed to.

Mr Cressman was an easy going man, a bit of a playboy, and although some years older than his new girlfriend, he wasn't ready to settle down. When he refused to respond to her prompting for a proposal on holiday in the south of France in the summer of 1999, he was doomed.

Guided by John Kelsey-Fry QC, Andrews told the Old Bailey jury her boyfriend was the violent one, who had beaten her and raped her. She had only hit out in self defence believing he was going to kill her, she said.

When it came to cross examination by Bruce Houlder QC, Andrews told of her tragic history of being a childhood victim of abuse and threw in the odd theatrical swoon, which needed the attendance of matron, to try and win the jury's sympathy.

It didn't work. They could tell a nasty piece of work intent on character assassination when they saw it.

Sentencing her to life imprisonment, the Recorder of London Michael Hyam QC told Andrews she had been "consumed with anger and bitterness."

Detective Chief Inspector Jim Dickie went further: "Andrews murdered Tommy Cressman in life and murdered his reputation in death," he said.

R. *v* Christina Guerrini and others

Liz Hurley – or Elizabeth Hurley as she liked to be known in the style of Elizabeth Taylor – was the hottest of the hot in 1995.

Her boyfriend Hugh Grant had just released Four Weddings and a Funeral and she had turned up at the premiere in THAT dress, the one with big safety pins and not much else.

She had also signed a £3 million contract to become the face of Estee Lauder and was all over the front covers of magazines and the front pages of the newspapers. And it was straight from a photoshoot for the cosmetics giant that she flew into Heathrow and was taken in a red BMW straight to Southwark Crown Court for an inconvenient date with the jury to describe how she had managed to be mugged by a bunch of teenage girls – or Liz Hurley and the burly girlies, as the tabloid papers put it.

Her arrival outside court was like the hysteria of a first night, but with less decorum and more free-for-all rugby-style brawling. More than 60 photographers hurled themselves into the melee as minders fought a path through and the star battled to look serene behind sunglasses on the gloomy March day.

Inside the court building Miss Hurley was quickly acquainted with typical court procedure – a three hour wait for legal argument to be played out. So a sideroom had to be found and a minder sent to the canteen for teas.

Eventually in mid-afternoon her cue came and Richard Onslow, proseucting, called the star witness. Every single eye was fixed on the court door and they waited … and waited. In classic Hollywood style Miss Hurley was not going to be rushed for her close-up. At last she glided in, dressed in a short black jacket and tight trousers, and in beautiful tones she spoke of being surrounded in the street near the home she shared with Grant in Little Boltons, Kensington the previous November.

The gang had threatened her and taken £10 and a number of unspecifed photographs, she said.

It was straight forward evidence, but being a star she could not let her moment in the witness box pass without a delightful Luvvie moment. Asked exactly how long the entire incident had taken she replied that she would have to relive it in her mind there in court. So saying she shut her eyes and entered what looked like a transfixed state. Fortunately we didn't get the full performance with dramatic gestures and lines, but she was clearly living the part in her mind.

"That's it," she pronounced opening her eyes after about a minute, "however long that was." In the dock were Christina Guerrini, 18, and two other girls who could not be named because of their age. A further 17-year-old had pleaded guilty earlier.

The jury returned guilty verdicts and Judge Gerald Butler passed a variety of minor sentences then invited counsel to his chambers for a chat over what had been an unusual case.

Max Mosley *v* News International

There's something peculiarly British and public school about the idea of spanking and pleasure, something rather old fashioned and innocent, even Carry On. So it was that when FIA motor racing boss Max Mosley sued the *News of the World* and its parent company for breaching his right to privacy by filming him being whipped and whipping semi naked women, the nation could only laugh rather than worry about the serious issues of privacy and freedom of expression.

Mosley, the son of 1930s British fascist leader Sir Oswald Mosley, had been particularly upset by the allegation not that he liked being beaten, but that he had liked recreating a Nazi theme. He had sued the paper over its story and pictures headlined "F1 boss has sick Nazi orgy with five hookers" published in March 2008.

The five hour sado-masochistic marathon had indeed taken place at a Chelsea flat rented by Mosley and used by ladies who revelled in providing him with the pleasures he so enjoyed. But even though they played prison camp guards and inmates and beat each other ferociously while speaking in German accents, there were no Nazi connotations, he insisted. Indeed that Friday afternoon was only one of many different role playing sketches he had enjoyed and afterwards they would all sit down to a cup of tea and pleasant chit-chat about the whole experience.

What the newspaper editor Colin Myler (above) never expected was Mosley to come to court and admit everything about his secret pleasures when, until the paper had published, he had not even told Jean his wife of nearly 50 years. But shameless and defiant the qualified barrister turned international sporting head did just that and challenged Mark Warby QC, representing the *NoW*, to find fault in him and justify the paper's intrusion.

Yes he had been privately educated in Britain, France and Germany and yes from a young age he has always liked the thrill of corporal punishment among consenting adults and was happy to pay for it. His counsel James Price QC was able to call four of the ladies who provided such enjoyment for him and yes, they too, loved doing what they did.

Rarely has court 13 at the High Court seen such colourful activities described by the fearless participants with such candour. Being whipped is painful but better than going to the dentist, said one. Bondage is not depraved its fun and harmless erotica, said another.

When the paper's star witness who had secretly filmed the goings-on with a camera hidden in her bra was unfit to come to court, the game was up for the newspaper.

Mr Justice Eady sided heavily with Mosley's right to privacy and awarded him £60,000, although refusing his demands for exemplary damages. The judge tried to head off criticism that he was gagging proper investigative journalism, insisting he was not making a landmark judgement, but Fleet Street editors thought otherwise and almost universally attacked him.

R. *v* Laurence

Slough – made famous by Betjeman's appeal for friendly bombs and Ricky Gervais's *The Office* – received another unwanted tag in November 2002 as the scene for Princess Anne to become the first member of the Royal Family to acquire a criminal record.

The splendour of Windsor Great Park is far removed from East Berkshire magistrates court and the Princess Royal's hauty but pained expression betrayed how she was not enjoying her day out in this unloved town. The Princess pleaded guilty to the charge of keeping the dangerous dog which had bitten two children in the park.

For the occasion she chose a patriotic outfit of blue jacket, white blouse, red skirt with matching designer scarf knotted tightly around her throat. Entering court with husband Commodore Timothy Laurence and children Peter and Zara, she plonked her handbag down in front of her with a mighty thud and sat not in the dock but next to barrister Hugo Keith.

"Is your name Anne Elizabeth Alice Laurence?" asked the court clerk.

"It is," came the curt response.

"Is your address Gatcombe Park, Gloucestershire?"

"Yuh." So the tone was set from the off.

In a way the mundane facts of the case failed to match the drama of the royal presence. Anthony Smith, prosecuting, told the court a twelve-year-old boy and another aged seven were bitten by Dottie, a three-year-old English bull terrier when it suddenly charged at them as they played on their bikes. Their father tried to kick it away, the Princess apologised profusely and the children were left traumatised, in need of hospital treatment but not seriously injured.

District Judge Penelope Hewitt had the power to jail the defendant for up to six months, impose a £5,000 fine and order the destruction of the dog. She was hardly going to send the Princess to the Tower, and kept the penalty to a £500 fine, with an order for her to pay £250 compensation and £148 prosecution costs.

To the fury of the family of the victims, who had been given the anonymity of the courts, Dottie was reprieved, although placed under a contingent destruction order – the canine equivalent of a suspended death sentence.

But Dottie's owner had her dignity given another tweak as well. She had to undergo a masterclass retraining programme, along with, no doubt to her dismay, fellow dangerous dog owners with criminal records.

Fisher *v* Brooker

"We skipped the light fandango, turned cartwheels cross the floor, I was feeling kinda seasick, but the band called out for more."

Those haunting and utterly meaningless words, the whirling, swirling, soaring organ ... if there had been some suspiciously sweet smelling cigarette smoke in the air we could have been back in the Summer of Love.

In fact it was November 2006 and court 56 of the High Court where fifty-year-old barristers toe-tapped along to the old Procol Harum hit *A Whiter Shade of Pale*.

A Yamaha organ was positioned in the witness box to the delight of Mr Justice Blackburne – music and law graduate at Cambridge – who mused about reliving old times by playing it out of hours to study chords and melody structures.

Former band members Gary Brooker and Matthew Fisher were present too but sadly this was not a reunion but a bitter battle over £1 million of royalties.

Brooker had been officially credited as the composer with lyric writer Keith Reid of the song which sold more than 10 million copies since its release in May 1967. Belatedly, Fisher claimed now that he had been primarily responsible.

Through his counsel Iain Purvis, the 61-year-old classically-trained musician turned computer programmer, claimed the famous solo

introduction evoking Bach and the Baroque was his. Brooker's only contribution to the solo was the chord sequence, he said.

But Andrew Sutcliffe QC, for Brooker, said his client and Mr Reid had written the song before Fisher had even joined the band.

In a wonderful illustration of how works of art can be conceived in the seemingly most uninspiring surroundings, he told the court that Brooker had first played the basis of it to Fisher in his mother's front room after hearing Bach's *Air on a G String* in a Hamlet cigar TV advert.

The judge sided mostly with Fisher awarding him a 40% share of the musical copyright but only from the day he started his claim in May 2005.

This was less than Fisher had hoped because, the judge explained, while the organ solo was a "distinctive and significant contribution" it was outweighed by Brooker's overall input.

This still left the singer with a sizable legal bill. The judgement was, he relected ruefully, "a darker shade of pale for creativity in the music business."

But Brooker's mood lightened on appeal when he won back the right to his royalties, only to darken again when the Law Lords reimposed the original judgement in Fisher's favour.

Royal Courts of Justice Ct 61 Before Mr. Justice Peter Smith

John Baldwin QC and Mr. James Abrahams instructed by Arnold & Porter for the Defendant

Mr. Jonathan Rayner James QC for Baigent & Leigh and Mr. Andrew Norris instructed by Orchard Brayton Graham LLP

Da Vinci Code

Author Dan Brown in witness box questioned by Mr. Jonathan Rayner James QC on behalf of Baigent & Leigh v Random House

Baigent and Leigh *v* Brown and others

What was the *Da Vinci Code* trial actually all about? A legal fight for a writer's integrity and reputation, or a giant publicity stunt to boost book sales and Hollywood box office, or maybe it was just a load of old hokum? On the face of it author Dan Brown (above) was being sued for plagiarism and copyright theft for stealing ideas from the book *Holy Blood, Holy Grail*, written by Michael Baigent and Richard Leigh.

Brown's twist which made *The Da Vinci Code* such a money spinner was the suggestion that Jesus had married Mary Magdalen, had a child whose heirs married into a line of French kings and whose bloodline survives to the present day. The co-authors claimed he had stolen 15 core themes from their book which had been published 19 years before *DVC*.

Brown at 41 was the world's richest author with sales of the best-selling thriller alone topping £250 million and, to say the very least, Baigent and Leigh were not in that league. Their book was not only virtually unknown but was not a novel at all but purely non-fiction. One of the few things they had in common was a shared publisher. Random House published the *DVC* and the paperback version of *Holy Blood*.

Outside court both books were piling on sales thanks to the trial publicity. Both Brown and Baigent had new books in the pipeline and

the *DVC* Hollywood blockbuster, with Tom Hanks and Sir Ian McKellen, was just weeks away from release.

Inside court, the three week trial was also playing to full houses engossed in the debates on the Merovingian monarchy, the Knights Templar and the whole history of early Christianity and the sight of these very different characters giving evidence.

The happy Leigh was like an extra from *Easy Rider* with white moustache, dark glasses, long black hair and magnificent 70s-style sideburns,while Baigent sported the more conventional literary looks and swept back grey hair. Brown, every inch the successful WASP New Englander, described their claims as "completely fanciful". While acknowledging he had used many books for research, he had paid tribute to his rivals by creating the character Leigh Teabing – played in the film by Sir Ian – from an anagram of their names.

He was to spend three gruelling days in the witness box coming under particular pressure from Jonathan Rayner-James QC for the claimants.

The court was packed even more tightly for the judgement from Mr Justice Peter Smith who supported Brown and, for some reason, felt it necessary to insert his own code into the written ruling.

R. *v* Shipman

It was a trial which destroyed a nation's faith in its homely, wise, unquestionably trusted family doctors.

Harold Shipman was 53 when he came to trial at Preston Crown Court in October 1999. He looked kindly, caring and just the sort of man who was safe with your family's health.

Was there something in his eyes behind his beard and glasses which betrayed his real intent? If there was, hundreds of patients and their families and friends never saw it. Yet for more than 20 years Dr Shipman injected fatal doses of morphine into mostly elderly women for the thrill of wielding the power over life and death.

As Richard Henriques QC, prosecuting, said in his opening speech: "He killed so often he must have found the drama of taking life to his taste. He killed these patients because he enjoyed doing so."

It wasn't only the victims and their nearest and dearest who were taken in. A succession of coroners and their officers barely lifted an eyebrow even when sudden deaths on Shipman's patch were outstripping all other local GPs put together.

He was eventually charged with 15 murders in three years at his one-man practice in Hyde, near Manchester. Of the victims nine had been buried and six cremated. Those buried were exhumed and the previously unsuspected signs of murder were clear to see.

Shipman had covered his tracks by clumsily forging medical records and telling lies. He even forged the £400,000 will of 82-year-old Kathleen Grundy to try and make money out of murder. But this was to prove his downfall as her solicitor daughter Angela Woodruffe immediately sensed something was wrong and her inquiries led, belatedly, to the police investigation.

In a powerful performance in the witness box Mrs Woodruffe told of how the life of her "dynamic and active" mother was suddenly extinguished after a visit by Dr Shipman and how she was then confronted by a badly-typed will which left the entire estate to the doctor, disinheriting herself and her two sons whom her mother had doted on.

Through the weeks of damming evidence Shipman sat impassive, occassionally glancing towards his loyal wife Primrose who came to court every day and believed unwaveringly in his innocence. If he shared that belief he never entered the witness box to justify it.

Mr Justice Forbes imposed 15 life sentences and recommended he should never be released.

Four years later he was found hanged in his cell in Wakefield prison but inquiries into his true death toll continued. At first the number of his victims was put at 215 covering his time as a GP between 1975 and 1998. Then it was officially raised to 250 by an inquiry covering his time as a junior hospital doctor as long ago as 1971.

R. *v* Bourgass and others

He was skinny with a weasel face and he was an utterly ruthless terrorist. Kamel Bourgass, the first Premier League al-Qaeda killer to come before a British court, was an Algerian graduate of the terror training camps of Afghanistan.

He entered Britain illegally in the back of a lorry from Calais and headed for the Finsbury Park mosque, then under the evil influence of Abu Hamza. Swiftly he assembled a poison production unit in a Wood Green flat aimed at spreading ricin and other deadly toxins across London.

When police raided the flat they found recipes, equipment and some of the raw materials to makes hundreds of lethal doses of ricin, cyancide and botulinum. They rounded up the suspects but Bourgass had fled. To the surprise of the police and security services he surfaced again in Manchester during a raid on other al-Qaeda suspects in the tatty Crumpsall Lane area.

Uniformed officers had been sent along as back up with no warning about the danger they might face. As they helped in the search of the small flat for evidence about their original targets, Bourgass seized a kitchen knife and in a explosion of violence killed one unprotected PC and stabbed and slashed three others. The seemingly frail figure was finally subdued but it was too late for PC Stephen Oake.

In a classic case of shutting the stable door, Bourgass who had been allowed to sit alone in the Manchester flat, was surrounded by six prison officers in full body armour when he appeared in the dock at the Old Bailey for a preliminary hearing.

When the case came to trial, Crown counsel Nigel Sweeney QC outlined the facts to two separate juries hearing first the murder and secondly the poison plot.

Mr Justice Penry Davey sentenced Bourgass, 31, to life imprisonment with a minimum of 22 years for the murder with further concurrent sentences totalling 38 years.

The second case, which concluded in April 2005, was less than straightforward. Michel Massih QC again represented the killer but, thanks to a total blackout on reporting, the jury had no knowledge of the first trial. Bourgasss was in the dock with four others arrested in or connected to the North London flat.

Their lawyers claimed the four had been caught up in something they knew nothing about. They also argued that the whole terrorist threat had been exaggerated as a political stunt to bolster PM Tony Blair's shaky authority.

The jury cleared the four of all charges and convicted Bourgasss not of plotting murder, but merely the lesser charge of conspiracy to cause a public nuisance. As a result four further terrorist suspects had their charges dropped before their trial due to start the next week.

Bourgass was sentenced to another 17 years.

Two months later four al-Qaeda terrorists detonated bombs killing 52 people on the Tube and a London bus, suggesting the terrorist threat was a little more real than the complacent or naive in the trial had believed.

R. *v* Kray

It was almost like a scene from *Alice Through The Looking Glass*, where everything is back to front.

In June 1997 Charlie Kray stood before the jury and swore blind that his twin brothers, Ronnie and Reggie, were nice, kind-hearted people not violent gangsters. He was a nice man too and totally against drugs, he said, so it was the police's fault he offered undercover officers cocaine worth £38 million and supplied them with 2 kgs as a starter.

Kray was 70 years old as he hobbled from the dock to the witness box in Woolwich Crown Court.

Twenty-eight years earlier he had been sentenced to ten years for helping to dispose of the body of Jack "the hat" McVitie, after he had been shot and stabbed through the eye by Reggie. More than a dozen members of the Kray gang had been sent down for their varied roles in their East End racqueteering of the 1960s, which included Ronnie's murder of George Cornell.

Since then Charlie had earned, and blown, £100,000 for his work as a consultant on the film *The Krays*, which glorified the family's violence, although his late mum Violet didn't approve of it and had been in touch through a psychic to say so, he said.

Now it was time to set the record straight.

The whole gangster blood and violence image was wrong when you got to know the twins. Ronnie was moody because of his mental illness, and Reggie just went off the rails when his wife Frances died.

Apart from that they would help anyone. As their older and more responsible brother, he had done his best but he couldn't watch them all the time, he continued, at times tearfully.

Nowadays he was nothing more than a washed-up old hasbeen reduced to "cadging" off rich people who wanted to hear his exaggerated reminiscences of "the good old days."

The sense of a fantasy world was enhanced when Jonathan Goldberg QC, defending, compared Kray senior to Lady Bracknell's reckless nephew Algernon, who "has nothing but looks everything." Character witnesses appeared of the calibre of "Mad" Frankie Frazer and James Nicholson, the Fleet Street veteran known as "the Prince of Darkness."

Reality returned when Judge Michael Carroll sentenced him to twelve years, saying the jury had clearly believed that his claims to hate drugs and dealers had been "hypocrisy."

Charlie didn't see out his sentence and died three years later in a hospital on the Isle of Wight soon after being moved from Parkhurst prison. Reggie had been transferred to Parkhurst from Wayland in Norfolk to be closer to his brother and was to die himself within a few years. Ronnie had died of a heart attack in Broadmoor in 1995.

Iselworth Crown Court Before Judge John Crocker
REM Peter Buck Trial   Air Rage Trial   Prosecutor David Bate QC
April 2002   Defended by Richard Ferguson QC
              and Trevor Burke QC

REM band members Michael Stipe and Michael Mills

R. *v* Peter Buck

He was six foot two inches tall, heavily built, 45 years old and tearing round the first class cabin of a BA Transatlantic Jumbo overturning a trolley and smashing crockery in a drunken air rage rampage.

When the captain left the flight deck to calm him Peter Buck shouted: "You're just a f****** captain, but I'm REM!"

It sounded like a familiar scene of a millionaire lead guitarist used to getting his way in a world famous rock band. But when his case came to trial at Isleworth Crown Court he spoilt all the old rock dinosaur stereotypes by apologising and blaming sleeping pills. Even worse his REM mates were called to tell the jury that Buck was a "southern American gentleman" and "not an alcoholic by American standards".

Buck stood before the court in March 2002 charged with being drunk on an aircraft, two counts of common assualt on cabin crew and one of criminal damage.

David Bate QC, prosecuting, told how the musician had gone on the rampage after drinking 18 glasses of red wine in three hours on a Seattle to Heathrow British Airways flight.

Witnesses described him trying to steal more wine from the galley, attempting to insert a compact disc into a catering trolley believing it to be a CD player, trying to slip a knife up his sleeve and being pulled away from the plane's door yelling "I want to go home" at 35,000 ft.

Buck, now soberly dressed in dark suit and tie, told the jury he had taken a sleeping tablet called Ambien he heard about at the Prince's Trust concert for Nelson Mandela in Trafalgar Square a few days before the flight in April 2001. He drank some red wine with it and the next thing he remembered was waking up in what he thought was a hospital ward in Disneyland but turned out to be a police cell.

He successfully came over as shy and non-confrontational, and his enormous legal team headed by Richard Ferguson QC and Trevor Burke QC, produced band co-members Michael Stipe and Mike Mills to confirm his niceness. Stipe even told how his friend would prefer to retire to his hotel room with a good book after a gig rather than join fellow band members in the bar.

Buck was cleared of all charges – even welcomed to fly again by BA – and left court arm in arm with Stipe, Mills and his wife Stephanie, a Seattle lawyer and restauranteur.

Justice had been done but at the cost to those who like their rock and roll legends to live up to a real old fashioned rock and roll reputation.

Lucasfilms *v* Ainsworth

In April 2008 Michael Bloch QC went into battle at the High Court not just with legal texts and his renown advocacy skills but some of the fiercest fighters of the universe.

Either side of him stood a full size Stormtrooper and a fighter pilot from the forces of Emperor Palpatine. On a table in front of him was a collection of helmets designed for conflict in far-off galaxies and the head of a Tusken Raider from the planet Tatooine.

For Mr Bloch was representing George Lucas, the creator of the *Star Wars* phenonemon, the Hollywood blockbusters which have spanned three decades and landed him an estimated $3.5 billion dollars from the films and related merchandise.

It was the costumes and paraphenalia which had brought this interplanetary hokum before Mr Justice Mann.

Lucasfilms was suing British engineer Andrew Ainsworth, who had helped to produce Stormtrooper suits and helmets for the first *Star Wars* film released in Britain in 1977. He had been paid for his efforts but in 2004 he discovered one of the originals in a cupboard and set about making some more to market commercially.

Lucas successfully sued him in California in 2006 and Mr Bloch was seeking to enforce that ruling in Britain – with the aid of his props.

Gesturing before him as he opened proceedings, he told the judge: "The gentlemen in the front row, who will be known no doubt to millions of people all round the world, are the subject matter of the entire case." Not wishing to assume too much prior judicial knowledge of the art form, he added: "As far as we know they are half human and half cloned warriors known as stormtroopers. What we are dealing with are characters of the imagination."

But not just mere imagination: "We would say the the stormtrooper helmet and armour both complete one of the most iconic images in modern culture", he added, granting them an equal status in law to Cyclops from classical mythology.

One thing was puzzling the judge, however. One of the stormtroopers "looked a bit more cross than others," he suggested. Mr Bloch replied that he was unsure "how a Stormtrooper expresses anger" and with no one in court – human, half cloned or otherwise – prepared to hazard a guess, the question remained unanswered.

Alistair Wilson QC, for Mr Ainsworth, claimed that the copyright on the Stormtrooper's form has expired because it was a piece of industrial design rather than a work of art. He also argued that there had been no formal contract between the parties.

In his ruling the judge confirmed that Lucasfilms had owned the rights and their copyright had been breached in the United States.

Index